DEVON

ISLAND

CANADA'S ROSWELL

By

S. Jonas Black

Dedicated to Dr. Joseph Red

Edited by P.J.K. (with much appreciation)

Index

Preface

Part One

Chapter 1	Life on the DEW line
Chapter 2	What is that?
Chapter 3	Discovering the wreck
Chapter 4	PPCLI called in
Chapter 5	First Contact
Chapter 6	I would like to buy a tent
Chapter 7	More equipment please
Chapter 8	Take the craft
Chapter 9	CFB Suffield, Canadas Area 51
Chapter 10	The dismantling
Chapter 11	Welcome to your new home

Part Two

Chapter 12	Project Overshot
Chapter 13	Secrecy kept
Chapter 14	Welcome Aboard
Chapter 15	Promotion for the Major
Chapter 16	Decisions, decisions…
Chapter 17	Road Trip
Chapter 18	Goodbye Lt. Col.

Part Three

(Transcripts of Interviews)

Chapter 19	Cpl. Ron Kaye
Chapter 20	Lt. Col Logan
Chapter 21	Maj. Stefanic
Chapter 22	Brig. Gen. A. Mouldy
Chapter 23	Cpt. F (Black Cloud) Engle
Chapter 24	Sgt. B W (Moose) McIntyre

DEVON ISLAND – CANADAS ROSWELL

Preface

For those of you who are not familiar with me or my work, I write under the pseudonym of 'S. Jonas Black'. Some people even feel he (S. Jonas Black) may be my alter ego. He might just be. In addition to writing books under my alter ego, I also have a YouTube channel and blog whereby I use my real name.

My blog and my show centers around government conspiracies and secrets kept from its citizens (both the citizens of Canada and the United States too). My guests are free to reveal anything they would like while I interview them for the blog and YouTube show. They know that there is no anonymity when they appear on my show, so they say only what they choose to say on that show. But when I put information in a book, I don't want anyone to be able to track down my source for information for the data I publish. Therefore, I do not release certain information on the blog or YouTube channel. That way the government doesn't attempt to locate my sources. Instead I write under my pseudonym to protect the informants who provide me with the information that I write about in my books. I will never breach their trust as I want, no need, to keep the information coming in for my books and shows.

It was in my first book, 'The Trifecta Papers', where I talked about the many steps I take to protect my informants. I also used my pseudonym for their protection as well as my own. Nothing has changed in this book as far as the steps I take to protect those who risked so much to give me the information I need. I hope the reader understands the importance of protecting these courageous people who risk so much to tell us their stories. Without them, I would not have been able to document their stories here for you to read.

I have conducted several interviews with several people to assist me in writing this book. I am attempting to write this as if I am the one observing it in person and in real time, as I feel this will most accurately reflect not only the incidents but the emotions regarding these specific events. What you are reading is real. The people are real. The only thing that is not real is their names. Some of the original witnesses have passed on, and some of the others are reluctant to talk. There are a few I could not locate. But the ones that I could locate and did talk to me gave me great information. I will be protecting their identities by not providing their real names.

The spacecraft described in this book is exactly as it was described to me by the witnesses. Although there were subtle differences amongst the various witnesses, for the most part they were all in agreement. I feel that the subtle differences lend itself to the overall credibility as it verifies that there was no collusion of the people involved. Sadly, some of the witnesses have passed on as it was over half a century ago.

During the interviews I learned what had happened to the aliens, as well as a good number of the soldiers who worked on this project. When the last of the aliens had died and the project ended, I know that the craft along with all the tools, documents, photos, alien cadavers, etc. where all moved to a secure storage facility that I have no idea where it is located. If anyone who reads this book knows please let me know as I would love to learn the whereabouts.

I can tell you that Lieutenant Colonel Logan (not his real name) is now an older man enjoying his retirement. He has a beautiful home overlooking the ocean. His mind is still sharp, and I have developed a good friendship with him. He is a good man, and a caring man. In some ways, he is the best 'man' I have ever had the pleasure of meeting.

Although my time in the military did overlap with some of the timeline covered in this book, I personally had no knowledge of any of it when I was in the military. I sure wish I had. The experiences those involved in it were so amazing.

So, I hope the following information is interesting to you, and like my first book, if you have any knowledge on this project that you feel would be of interest or informative to the reader, please send it to me for further revisions of this book.

PART ONE

Chapter One

'Life on the DEW Line'

The DEW (Distant Early Warning) line ran from Greenland through Canada to Alaska in the arctic. It was started in 1957 although the planning and building began a few years earlier. Most of the DEW line was located in Canada in the far north with some of it located in both Greenland and Alaska. It consisted of several radar installations monitoring long range bombers from the USSR (Union of Soviet Socialist Republic). They also monitored the launching of ICBMs or Intercontinental Ballistic Missiles. These sites are staffed by both Canadian and American Air Force soldiers with NORAD (North America Aerospace Defence) assuming overall command. This system remained in place for several years until replaced in 1993 by a more automated system.

Along the DEW-line on September 27th 1966, Ron Kaye was sitting at his monitoring post in the warm building that made up part of PIN-4. Jim Reeves was performing Distant Drums as it was coming over Radio Canada International on the shortwave radio next to his desk. Later at 1800 Zulu time, he would listen to the world news on BBC shortwave. The day before there was a light snow outside that Ron often jokingly called a 'powder puff' (He used this term regardless of how heavy the snow really was). Today it was clear outside, and the sun is shining for about eight hours a day.

Ron had been in the air force for a few years. His actual occupation was as an instrumentation technician. This Dew-Line location was staffed by a team of six to eight people. Ron was on his second deployment in the far north. Here on the DEW-line they typically had one instrumentation technician, along with a radar technician, diesel mechanic and of course the radar operators (which they were all cross trained as well in other things). In addition to this, they all took turns being the stations cook as well as covering off all the other station duties and chores, of which there were many.

PIN-4 was their section of the DEW line and it is a remote outpost located on Victoria Island. The DEW- line had been in place a few years and ran roughly along the 69th Parallel. At this time of the year, the window of daylight was rapidly getting closed. Soon the sun would set for the winter. It was a welcomed time as there were fewer Soviet spy planes entering in the dark. The number of bomber runs remained unchanged in the dark though. Long range Soviet bombers would often cross into Canadian territory but would hustle back before they were intercepted by the CF-101 fighter interceptors that the Canadian Air Force used then. Spy planes didn't fly as much in the dark as there was less to take pictures of. Unless they fly further south, but that was very risky for Soviet Spy planes to do so.   Each kilometer further south increased the chance that an interceptor plane would catch up to them. They didn't want to be shot down and the memory of Francis Gary Powers being shot down in May of 1960 in his U2 spy plane was still fresh in everyone's mind. This was especially true by the pilots of spy planes on both sides of the cold war.

The CF-101 fighter interceptor plane was manufactured by McDonnell Aircraft Corporation and suited for use in the arctic. Typically, they were deployed out from Canadian Forces Base Cold Lake in Alberta; they could reach the DEW-line in just over one hour. They were first introduced into service in 1961 and the last of them were finally retired in 1987. The pilots who flew them affectionately referred to them by their shortened name of the "Voodoo". The Voodoo was brought in to replace the Avro Canada CF101 affectionately called the Canuck which entered service with Canada in 1950 and was fully retired by 1981. This was the only Canadian-designed fighter to enter mass production.

Just a few years before, Avro Canada had announced the Arrow aircraft on the same day that the USSR had launched Sputnik, October 4th 1957. Sadly the Arrow program was cancelled for political reasons. It was speculated that the Arrow would have been the best military fighter, interceptor and small bomber for many years. Some aviation experts say that it would still to this day be the best aircraft for arctic interception. But the 'Voodoo' is what we had at that time. Many of the engineers working for Avro went on to work for either NASA or other American aviation companies.

Ron Kaye or Corporal Kaye as was his title in the air force was enjoying a hot coffee with the high frequency radio playing music in the background. He often tuned his Hallicrafter shortwave set to different stations when he was on his shift. Off shift he would switch on the Collins transceiver he brought with him and make ham radio contacts. Of course, he would never tell the other amateur radio operators that he was on the DEW-line, as that was strictly forbidden. Ron was pretty relaxed now that he had spent considerable time in front of the radar screen. When he first arrived there and he saw a huge mass on the radar's CRT display, he was certain that it was a large bomber in North American air space. One of the other radar operators calmly walked to his screen and started laughing.

"I too have been caught by that sort of thing. It is nothing more than a large flock of snow geese making their way south. They are a little late though; usually they pass by here a week earlier." John Watts was the Sargent in charge of PIN-4. He was a bit of a loner by nature, and he was well suited the remote work of a DEW-Line worker. There was a little bit of an inside joke having a radar technician with the last name of Watts. And yes, the others at that station teased him about that. But it was all in fun as he was well respected by the others.

Today though, Corporal Kaye was far more seasoned and felt he could identify nearly all common aircraft and flocks of birds by the 'signature' they left on his screen. As he was leaning back in his chair listening to music now coming from "Voice of America" on the outposts' Hallicrafter, a green blip caught his attention. Sitting upright and turning his chair over to the screen he could immediately discern that it was not a flock of geese. Calibrating the screen and counting the time between the blip and the white lines painted on the screen quickly suggested that it was a large fast moving plane. The radar signature and direction of travel indicated that it was likely a Soviet Tupolev Tu-95 which was a long-range heavy bomber. Of course, they had no legitimate purpose entering North American air space, other than the usual intimidation or the remote possibility of an actual attack on the United States or Canada. It was unlikely they would drop any bombs, but every one of these entries into Canadian air space needed to be taken seriously, and they were.

Ron picked up the handset for the Harris Radio linked to all other Dew-Line stations as well as the base in Cold Lake and the Canadian NORAD headquarters located at Canadian Forces Base Winnipeg. A report was made that they have a "hot one" coming south and could they send a couple Voodoos to intercept.

The pilots and ground crew at Canadian Forces Base Cold Lake had deployment down to a fine art. From the time the call came in, they could have two planes on the runway in eight minutes. Two minutes later they were heading north.

As with most Soviet pilots, this captain of the TU-95 knew exactly how far south he could get before he had to turn around and head back towards Soviet airspace. He flew south for just under one more hour, which put him well into Canadian Airspace. This was something these pilots were well aware they were doing. If the pilot preceded any further south, the CF-101's would catch up and could potentially shoot them down. Of course, there could also be the rare chance that a pilot and crew were 'defecting'. But that was highly unlikely although not impossible. In the case that the plane had indicated intention for defection, the CF-101's would divert the TU-95 to a very remote air strip. There was always the fear that it could be a suicide mission and once the plane is on the ground, its nuclear weapons could be detonated. This would also give the Soviet Union the ability to deny having anything to do with this attack. The blame could be put on rogue pilots or crew who changed their mind about defecting. That is why there was a remote air strip created for just this purpose. Also, this way the damage and loss of life on the ground would be minimal.

Ron was watching as the Tupolev was getting closer and closer to the station. He was not concerned with being seen by the plane; at his altitude it was very unlikely the radar station would be visible at this plane's altitude. Besides it was likely that Soviet intelligence knew where every DEW-line building was located. Ron thought of stepping outside if it was a clear enough sky to see if the plane could be spotted, but he knew he should not leave his post. Also, today was overcast, so there was no reason to look. He had never actually seen a TU-95 but always wanted to. He had an interest in different planes. Also, it was unlikely the plane had its navigation lights on.

With the next sweep on the radar screen, Ron spotted two close dots. They were so close they looked more like one sideways rectangle. They were coming up from the bottom of the screen indicating to him that they were coming from the south. After a few adjustments later and those two dots where confirmed to be the Voodoos he requested. Expanding his screen settings back out, he noticed the Tupolev TU-95 start on a banking turn to head back north. Once the turn is completed the CF-101 Avro's would take a much longer time to close the gap. A quick calculation from the calibrated painted lines showed that by the time the Voodoos did catch up, the Soviet bomber would be well out of Canadian Airspace and likely even in Soviet airspace. This Soviet pilot was good. He knew clearly how far he could enter Canadian air space before turning around. Ron made another call to Cold Lake to give an updated situation report. There was almost no reason have the CF-101 pursue the Soviet Bomber, but the procedure is to keep them in the air for some time in case the TU-95 turned around again, but that had never happened before. However, one half turn left or right could keep the Tupolev in Canadian airspace much longer.

Ron really enjoyed the periodic excitement that this job offered him, but no job is done until all the paperwork is completed (which was a common saying in the military), so he started to fill out the appropriate log sheets and reports to be sent in on the mail run. Military reports were common place. Mostly they just filled out a log, but in the case that an interception was requested, there was a separate form. Mostly just date and time plus what occurred. Of course, the report could not be finished until after the Soviet plane was off his screen, but starting it was always wise. After about forty-five more minutes, the Tupolev had finally left the screen to the North. The CF-101's continued north for a few more minutes before turning south to begin their flight back to CFB Cold Lake.

Now that the Canadian planes were heading south, Ron could now complete his paperwork; Sargent Watts came in and took his now cold coffee away from his desk. A few minutes later he returned with a full one that was steaming hot and placed it next to him, along with some cookies his wife had previously mailed up to him. It was small things like this helped to keep the morale high in remote locations.

"Thank you, John. I was so engrossed in watching the TU-95 and our Voodoos that I forgot to enjoy my coffee." Military formality was not a huge issue in these remote locations. Sure there was still rank and someone in charge, but if everyone did their job, rank was rarely an issue. Sargent Watts reviewed the report and signed it off. It was pretty straightforward.

"Ron, in less than two weeks if the weather gives us a good window, a CC-130 will be doing a low altitude drop of supplies and mail for us." The Lockheed CC-130 was a transport plane that was used for everything from soldiers, to cargo, to parachutists for the airborne regiment. Although there is a long-standing joke in the military that says, 'why would anyone want to jump out of a perfectly good plane?'

"Let's hope they get the drop a little closer this time. Last month they were over one click away." No one wanted to carry items from the drop zone back to their buildings, so when it was far away, it was even worse. Sometimes it was even several trips back and forth from the buildings.

The drop time was always a good time for the remotely located staff at any DEW line outpost. Mail and packages would arrive, as well as fresh rations that would last a couple weeks, then back to the canned goods. John's wife would often bake cookies and get them to the airstrip in time for the flight out. John knew that by him sharing them, everyone would be happy. Besides, the other staff often shared the treats they received from home. Ron received regular pouches of hard candies because his girlfriend Lynn could not bake very well. But that was okay for Ron; he loved the scotch mints she sent him. He was often teased about being the only one who could like mints while serving in the far north. But Lynn could also knit, and she enjoyed making wool neck scarfs for Ron and the others at his remote outpost. They all appreciated to too. They knew if the weather prevented an air drop from a plane, they would need to ration the fuel and turn the heat down amongst other things. So, the scarfs were a treasured item. The arctic clothing the airmen were issued is just too warm to be worn indoors.

These supply drops with the packages always improved the morale at these isolated stations, but overall, the morale was very good; not only in PIN-4 but in most of these locations. Generally speaking, the staff enjoyed their rotations to the DEW-line. The staff would do about eight months there and rotate out, yet most were eager to sign up for another eight months. The pace was relaxing, yet just enough excitement to keep you involved. The remote location offered slightly better pay, and with nothing there to spend your money on, you could really save up. Many would come home and purchase a new fancy car right off the lot. Ron was more interested in saving his money, preferring a simpler life.

Chapter Two

(What is that?)

It started out to be a typically uneventful shift on the DEW-Line back on October 4th 1966. The sun was nearly set for the season, showing itself for only a couple hours a day now. Ron Kaye sat down at the start of his usual shift and conducted the usual preliminary radar test that all operators do at the start of their day. Everything appeared as it should and there was nothing of interest displaying on the screen. Other than the usual aircraft which was often flying across his screen, Ron could see a Boeing 707 flying from the area of Greenland. That was currently the largest aircraft displayed. Although the DEW-Line didn't have typical flight transponder receivers, he could tell from the radar signature that it was likely a 707 and from the direction it was traveling it had left England. Besides, if it came from another area, a different DEW-line or PIN location would have spotted it. The DEW-line systems did have a system called IFF which stood for 'Identification Friend or Foe' first developed in World War Two to assist in spotting enemy aircraft.

Only a few minutes later, with no warning at all, a bright and large signal appeared on the top of the display. Ron looked down and saw immediately that it was the largest radar return he had ever seen. Adjusting the knobs, he zoomed in on that blip and measured it at approximately three hundred meters across. He thought it must be either a malfunction or a huge flock of geese. But geese do not move this quickly. Nothing this large had ever been seen before. His first thought after ascertaining the size of it, was to assume that it was some sort of new Soviet plane or weapon; one with massive proportions. Ron called for Sargent Watts attend the radar room in order to have a look at his screen, but before he arrived, he began re-running the test of the radar system. It checked out fine.

Corporal Kaye immediately began a second system test with slightly more comprehensive diagnostics. This second test took about two more minutes to conduct. This was precious time if it turned out to be hostile. Once again everything seemed fine. Sgt. Watts had already arrived and was watching over his shoulder in disbelief due to the massive size of the unknown object.

When John had first arrived, he was looking tired as it was the middle of the night due to the shift he was currently scheduled on. Now that he was alerted to this unknown object, he was suddenly wide awake. "What do you have on the screen?" He asked with a very confused tone to his voice.

"I do not have a clue. This is the biggest thing I have ever seen on this screen. I think it is over three hundred meters across"

"No way. This must be a system error. Let's have a look". John too did a quick systems test, despite having seen the in depth one done only moments before. All of the equipment appeared to be working as it should. He was even saw the in-depth check done right there in front of him. Still, something this large caused confusion to them both. Three of the four tests were likely done simply as a way to buy them some time to think about what to do next. They never had anything like this occur before. As John was double checking the calibration to re-estimate the size of this aircraft, Ron noticed that it was getting pretty close to the 707 approaching from the direction of Greenland in the East.

In 1966 the aviation industry did not yet have a working 'Traffic Collision Avoidance System or TCAS installed on commercial planes. These came about in the mid 1970's and implementation began in 1981. But even if it did, it was unlikely that a Russian military plane would have one, or if it did, it would have been deliberately turned off.

"John, are they on a collision course? They look like they are going to hit." The information on the radar screen was limited in certain information as it was not an air traffic controller screen. The altitude information was limited at best, but it did appear that they would merge over Devon Island. Both Corporal Kaye and Sargent Watts hoped there was enough altitude difference to ensure a safe distance between the two aircraft.

"Call Cold Lake now!" Barked the sergeant with some urgency in his voice. This was unusual for Sergeant Watts, he was usually a cool and quiet man, especially under pressure. This did not go unnoticed by Ron, who was now feeling the full urgency of this situation.

Ron called immediately on the Harris set, but before he could report his concern, the blips merged. The situation was reported to Cold Lake immediately. Unfortunately, the blip on the screen never returned to the two blips as hoped for. Instead there was just the one that appeared to be coming from Greenland. Ron's first thought is that whatever kind of big plane this was, it was possible they were hiding behind the 707 knowing it would show as only one dot on the screen. This was an old trick the Nazis did in World War Two to fool the British into thinking there were fewer planes than there really were. The British always anticipated this trick so the effect was minimal. But the size on this radar screen now was only the size of the original 707. What was going on here? It was not uncommon for military aircraft to sneak in behind the commercial aircraft so that only one radar image would be shown. Was this the case here? If so, why was the image the size of the 707 and nothing more? Still they had to assume the unknown plane was following the 707. Nothing else seemed to fit.

The Canadian Forces Base in Cold Lake Alberta promptly responded that they would be sending up two Voodoos right away. After quite some time, the CF-101 Canuck's caught up with the Boeing 707 and snuck in behind them. It was not long after that when, they radioed back that there was just another commercial plane and nothing else. There was no sign of a heavy bomber or any other trailing aircraft of any sort. This information was of course was relayed back to PIN-4 without delay.

The two on shift at PIN-4 were stumped as to what this could be. Could an aircraft have crossed too close to the exhaust and it entered the intake and shut the engine down? Would it disappear that quickly? It was so far away that it could through the curvature of the earth be under the horizon with just a little drop in altitude. What had the other PIN sites seen? These were questions that the staff at this DEW-Line post suspected they would never know the answers to.

After the confirmation of no planes trailing the 707, the Avro aircraft were then re-directed to the point over Devon Island that the planes crossed paths. The 707 crew were contacted via commercial air traffic controllers to see if they had spotted a large plane during their flight. The commercial pilots of the Boeing replied that no other planes had been seen at all in the arctic. Although it was dark out, they would see the navigational lights as it was clear, and visibility was good. Of course, foreign aircraft improperly entering Canadian airspace would certainly have the navigation lights shut off, even though this is a dangerous practice.

Fearing that there may have been a mishap of a plane getting exhaust from the Boeing 707 sucked into the engine and causing an engine fail, the CF-101's were to fly low and slow over Devon Island. They were still about half an hour away. It was dark out, but it was clear, and the moon was just bright enough for the pilots of the Avro's to see the horizon.

As the Avros approached Devon Island, their altitude was about five thousand feet which was quite low considering the elevation of some mountains located on Devon Island. This Island resembled a bowl in shape, and the middle was actually lower altitude than the edges of the island. They were flying about as slow as you can safely go without a stall. A grid was flown to cover as much of the island as possible, but the pilots knew they could only cover a small percentage of the island before their fuel levels became too low to continue. Devon Island is huge; it is actually the 27th largest island in the world. So, the pilots would only see a tiny portion of the Island.

On the second pass of their grid, the pilot on the west of the two-plane formation noticed something on the ground that looked like a blue spotlight shining dimly from the ground towards the sky in a near straight up line. The two planes banked hard over to investigate as it was a distance away. What they then saw the two pilots will never forget; the image was burned into their memories forever. It was a craft shaped like a boomerang. Only this boomerang was 300 meters long or longer. It was massive. They observed it for several minutes to see if there were signs of life and to attempt to identify the craft or the numbering system to see where it was originating from. During this time, there was a fog like haze coming from underneath the boomerang craft. There were also dim lights shining out of it. In the fog there were places where they could see a dim pink light peeking out from underneath it. This made it much easier to spot from far distances, and if not for the mist like fog and the lights, the pilots would have likely flown right over it without spotting the aircraft.

The pilots knew not to discuss too much of their observation over the radio. But they said just enough to let their base know there was something big that needed to be investigated. Of course, they would have a full debriefing from the military intelligence section when they returned to their base in a couple hours. They anticipated this and it happened.

The CF-101 pilots now turned south and returned to base. Their fuel levels were good, but they could not stay much longer. Once landed, they were met on the tarmac as they stepped out of their planes. The two pilots were escorted inside an office where they proceeded to give full verbal reports on what they had seen. Not only did they need to verbally deliver their report, they also needed to file their standard written report. They were also interviewed by two officers from the intelligence section as they had anticipated they would be. The two pilots wondered if they had stumbled upon a new soviet long-range bomber. This could possibly one that had yet to be identified by NATO or CIA agents inside the USSR. And due to the massive size of this aircraft, it could be a game changer for protection of North American air space.

At the same time, the personnel at PIN-4 (Ron and John) were contacted by Winnipeg and told to write a full report on what they both saw. Each had to write their own comprehensive report and the instructions were that they were not to talk to each other or to collaborate on this report. They were then told not to relay it over their Harris set, but instead to place it in an envelope and sealed it as it was to be handed over to the Load Tech of the CC130 now scheduled to arrive the very next day. They both felt this must be very big to reschedule the arrival of the CC130 about one week early.

On October 5th 1966, landing a CC130 in the snow in the dark was no simple task. All staff had to be on shift with each person lighting flares along the path of the snow runway. As the plane normally takes off and lands on pavement, it needed to be fitted with skids for the snow landing. But this chore was done, and the pilots did this frequently enough that there was no issues and little concern.

The plane circled once to ensure the landing was from the correct direction and then it came in for its final approach. It actually managed to come to a stop fairly close to the PIN-4 stores building, so the cargo was quickly offloaded. The sealed envelopes with the reports from Ron and John were handed over to the load tech for his safekeeping.

The load tech is an integral part of a transport aircrafts crew. He is responsible for ensuring loads are properly balanced, within the weight limits, and he properly secured the cargo, so it does not shift while in flight. On this flight, the load tech was an air force corporal. He had a large envelope with him that he handed over to John and responded that it must be very important as he was told to guard this envelope like they are solid gold bars. But the corporal had known not to ask questions and simply secured the envelope in an inside jacket pocket as he raised the tail gate of the CC130 just before they taxied to where the makeshift runway was located.

He had also done the same with the envelopes previously handed over from John. He placed them in an inside zippered pocket and patted his jacket to show they were secure. The entire time on the ground was less than fifteen minutes, and the engines were never shut down. Now the PIN-4 crew had to move all the cargo inside. That may be a big chore, but with fresh rations, parcels, fuel and mail, they crew were happy to undertake this task. Despite the bitter cold, they task was one they gladly endured. And this time the cargo was close to their buildings.

The skids weighed too much to simply carry into the storage area of PIN-4, so the crew made a human chain to bring all the goods into the building. Even if they had a forklift, it would not work in the snow laden ground. During the short summer months, the ground would be too soft to allow a forklift to work. It may work in the dead of winter due to the ice layer, but it would be impractical to have one here at PIN-4.

In addition to the usual supplies delivered, there was another 20 barrels of diesel fuel. They must be stored indoors as it was possible for them to freeze in the cold arctic winters. Along with the fuel already on hand, they had enough fuel for four more months. It was always a good idea to have a couple more months than expected, as it is impossible to bank on the weather being good enough for future landings. The weather could potentially be bad for days of even weeks. Sometimes it was just a short opening where the weather would be suitable for a plane drop. Other supplies included bulk foods and fresh bread, mail and parcels, plus office supplies and spare parts for the radar station. They were well set for some time, assuming that nothing went seriously wrong. Two years prior something did go seriously wrong. In the dead of night, the generator ran out of fuel. Back then there was no overnight shift as the belief was that no planes would fly over at that time. When the generator shut off, the room started to get cold. It became so cold that the diesel fuel froze. When the sleeping quarters started getting cold, the staff awoke to discover what happened. They entered the generator building to restart it, but the fuel was thick like molasses. When it gets below minus eighteen degrees centigrade, the viscosity of the fuel becomes too thick to pump to the engine. The staff brought all the wooden furniture over to the concrete generator hut and started a fire to heat the diesel. They finally got the fuel warm enough to restart the generator after burning the last of their furniture. That was a very close call that nearly ended in their collective deaths. From this point on, there would always be someone on shift to ensure this never happened again.

So, this shipment of fuel and other supplies really was critical for their survival. Of course, the biggest boost to their morale was the mail and packages from home. As this shipment was unexpected, it was a real treat to receive letters from loved ones, fresh baked cookies, and other things needed. All these things made the remoteness of this Job and the months of light followed by months of darkness a little more bearable. Then John remembered the envelope the load tech handed him from headquarters. These usually contained documents like pay statements, routine orders, and the like. But not this time:

Sergeant Watts reviewed the documents carefully; he had never received documents quite like these before. At first, he said nothing, but after all the goods were properly stowed in the storage areas, he called everyone together in the radar monitoring room so that the radar observer, who was not assisting in the arrival of the cargo, could participate.

"I received an interesting envelope that was delivered by the CC130. It arrived from NDHQ (National Defence Headquarters – In Ottawa Ontario). This document is a set of non-disclosure forms due the large blip we saw on the radar just a few hours ago. They want each and every one of us to sign them even if you were off shift and asleep. It seems we are never to talk about this ever again, not even amongst ourselves. I have to say, this is very strange".

Ron asked; "John, what do you think that is about?"

"I suspect what we discovered was a new super huge Soviet bomber. Likely if the public learned of it, there could be some serious panic. I mean the size of the blip on the screen made it look like we could land our planes on it. It was huge. Imagine the weaponry it could carry?" Imagine the threat to both the US and Canada?

A silence fell among the staff as they each visualised the enormous aircraft the Soviets must have developed. Then they each took their specified document, read it over and signed their names to it, as well as witnessing the documents of the person next to them. They all agreed to never discuss it again. For the few hours, there was very little discussion at PIN-4, other than casual talk about their mail from home or sharing some baked goods.

Although there was no further talk about what was seen on the radar that day, both Ron and John started to wonder what that blip really was. Could it simply be a new extremely large long-range bomber or was it something much more ominous than that. No one could envision a three-hundred-meter-wide plane. Of course, whenever there is an imposed secrecy on these matters, it causes people to question events even more so. In their minds they did just that. Being the good citizens that they were, they tried not talk about it for the entire duration of their career with the Canadian Air Force, but curiosity got the better of them.

A couple days later, despite the orders for silence, they did discuss and speculate what it was they encountered. They had discussions about what the Soviets might have developed, how large it was, and what it could carry and for how far.

Chapter Three

'Discovering the wreck'

Unbeknownst to both Ron and John, and the remainder of PIN-4, or even to the Avro pilots, the Canadian Rangers were nearby on a hunt and dispatched to Devon Island within two hours of the Avros finishing their pass over Devon Island. The Rangers had to travel just a short distance over ice from north of Prince of Wales Island to Devon Island, a distance of under 250 kilometers which for the vastness of the Arctic, was not that far. Fortunately, these Canadian Rangers were conducting a seal and walrus hunt using skidoo's towing large sleds with all their gear. So, it was just a few hours travel North East to reach Devon Island. The real challenge was when they got to the shores. They needed to find a pathway to the top without their snow mobiles as Devon Island is an arctic desert. Once over the crest of the top, they proceeded to the area described to them. But Devon Island is huge. Therefore, traversing it would take considerable time. But as it had very little precipitation, the walk was not too difficult. Also, the crash site was reported to be at the south west area of the Island, so luck was on their side in regard to the amount of walking once they arrived on the island.

The Canadian Rangers are made up of volunteers who primarily reside in the remote areas of Canada. Every member was issued one Lee-Enfield rifle and 200 rounds of ammunition each year. These rifles were used mainly for hunting, but they knew their equipment well, they know the arctic even better and can survive in the worst weather the Canadian Arctic could throw at them.

The Lee-Enfield was a reliable bolt action rifle that chambered the .303 calibre round and held ten shots in the box magazine. First production started in 1895, (in Canada it was first adopted part way into the First World War and used right through to after the Korean War). This rifle was by far the most reliable one available for use in the far north. Canada had officially swapped out the Lee-Enfield for the FN-C1A1, a Canadian version of the FN-FAL back in the early to mid-nineteen fifties. The FN-C1A1 was a fantastic weapon, but unproven at that time for the sub-zero temperatures the far north experienced.

The Canadian Rangers loved their Lee-Enfields. They are great rifles that are extremely reliable and accurate. And the Rangers are good with them. Most could hit a bullseye from extreme distances. They attended training a couple times a year, but they were so good at sneaking up on their prey during the hunt, that they could teach the instructors a thing or two. And as they live in the arctic, they also knew how to survive in these conditions with little difficulty. In addition, the Inuit people were generally a very happy group of people; even in adversity they tend to maintain their positive attitudes. Life in the far north was not easy, but they made the best of it all while maintaining a fantastic attitude.

Finally, after a period of considerable traveling, the small crew of Canadian Rangers were on Devon Island and searching for a way over the top of the coastal ridge to begin conducting their hunt for the downed plane. They quickly determined that it could take days to properly search just a small corner of this huge island. What they did not know was the vast size of the craft they were searching for and the lights emanating from it. They had to abandon their skidoos near the edge of the island as the snow and ice was not thick enough for their skidoos. Also, there was no clear path to bring them past the coastal ridges. So, they traversed the ridge on foot.

As they proceeded north east across the island, starting from the south coast, they were walking on bare rock; which had the effect of drawing the heat out of their feet. Frostbite was a real concern here. Snow was much better to walk on for keeping your feet warm. The rocks could prove to be life threatening.

After only about half an hour of walking after getting over the crest of the hills surrounding the island, luck was on their side when one noticed a faint light coming from the ground and shining towards the sky. Although it was not very bright, it was still visible in the cold clear air. It was morphing colours between green and orange. It was still some distance away, but they now knew where to go now, and that was a huge success and a major break in cutting down the time needed for searching.

After quite some time of walking, the small crew of Canadian Rangers neared the downed craft. Fear took over their bodies as they could not comprehend what they were seeing. This this thing was massive. Well over the radar estimate of 300 meters. The Rangers estimated it at over 450 meters in a boomerang shape. From the center tip to either end of a wing it was at least 225 meters long, but they had nothing to measure it with. In addition to that, it was dark out and difficult to see the entire craft. They couldn't risk using their flashlights.

One of the rangers removed his backpack and took out his Spilsbury SSB radio. This tiny radio was manufactured in Vancouver British Columbia, for use in terrain much like this. Spilsbury was one of the first companies to build portable High Frequency transceivers for non-military use. Most users claimed this civilian radio company had better equipment than the military purchased and provided.

The Ranger strung out the wire antenna and radioed in what he was seeing. The ranger, who grew up and spent his entire life in the arctic, had never seen a plane anything like this one before. He was surprised to hear the voice on the other end instructing him to stop speaking at once about this. He did receive instructions to have him and his crew protect the craft while more staff was dispatched.

The Rangers sent half their crew back to the sleds to retrieve as much equipment as could be carried. Still it took several trips to bring everything over. It was also a long hike to and from their skidoos. The remainder of the crew kept a watch on the plane in the event that the pilots and air crew emerged.

Chapter Four

PPCLI Called in

The Canadian Army had a base in Calgary, called "Canadian Force Base (CFB) Calgary." It was only months after being amalgamated from two other bivouacs. The Sarcee barracks and Currie Barracks now made up the new CFB Calgary bivouac. Staffed with members from Three PPCLI (Princess Patricia's Canadian Light Infantry), or often shortened to Princess Pats (plus an assortment of other shortened names, some nice, some not), these soldiers made up one of the larger infantry battalions in all of Canada.

Although this base was nowhere near the closest one to Devon Island, they had two CC130's nearby and the Calgary airport, and there were soldiers trained in Arctic Warfare currently on hand. This caused the base to handle the general alert that came out for forty of their soldiers to prepare for immediate deployment. Captain Douglas (Doug) Logan was the officer in charge of these forty men. He was well liked and respected by his subordinates.

Captain Logan was told that there was likely a new Soviet bomber that went down, and his objective was to capture it and any nukes that may be on board. In addition, if there were survivors, they would need to be taken as prisoners. There was a risk that they may detonate the nukes to keep from being captured, so this was considered a serious and imminent mission. Ideally, there would be survivors and they would be captured unharmed. But if they required medical attention, they would get the best treatment available. This would be done so that if Canadian personnel were ever captured, the hope would be that the Soviet Union would do the same.

Their Kit was quickly drawn from base supply. The weapons along with ammunition were issued from stores, and in less than two hours they were making their way to their plane sitting fueled up and ready to go on the tarmac at Calgary International Airport. The other plane was still being loaded with drop pallets by other staff from the base. The plane could touch down at a slow air speed and deploy the pallets and then get airborne again within seconds. But in this case, there was no place to do that, so they would be deployed with a parachute. With their backpacks, weapons and chutes, they were well weighed down. But they had experience doing these many times before in practice.

The flight from Calgary to Devon Island took a few hours as the transport plane is not a particularly fast plane. Also, it was not a comfortable flight, but they didn't sign up for comfort and they had great attitudes about this sudden deployment. Many assumed it was just a drill or at most a benign event. Even Captain Logan thought it might be just that. Still they would treat it as a real mission. You can never be sure of the outcome of these last-minute situations, and if it was a drill, they all knew they would be viewed on the effectiveness of their work.

Despite the fact that it was mid-day, the sun was down this far north, so it would be just like doing a night time jump. The signal was given to prepare for the jump. One by one each soldier checked their chute and then checked their buddies' chute. They then clipped their static lines to the plane to automatically deploy their chutes upon exit from the plane. A fifteen-foot tether was hanging below them to their back packs so that when they felt the weight come off, they knew they were about to hit the ground.

Within about two minutes they were all safely on the ground. Five minutes later, their chutes were bundled, and they awaited the arrival of the next CC130 with their supplies. Fortunately, the next plane saw the faint light coming from the boomerang shaped object and made the drop even closer to the downed craft. This saved the soldiers a considerable amount of time.

The soldiers then started their walk to find the Rangers and just as importantly the downed aircraft. Even at a far distance away, the darkness of the arctic it made the dim lights stand out and the soldiers didn't even require their compasses to take a bearing. Within half an hour they were at the suspected crash site.

When they arrived at the location, and they met with the Canadian Rangers, who challenged them with their rifles pointed in their general direction which is a standard procedure. Fortunately, this procedure and the challenge were responded to correctly and rifles were lowered. From this point on they would be working closely together. The PPCLI soldiers noticed this small group seemed almost scared of what was there. Certainly, they were on edge about this. Usually the Inuit were a very happy group. They may not behave like typical soldiers, but the work they did was invaluable to Canada and their service in the north, and every member of the Infantry knew it. It was commonly known that if it were not for these Canadian Rangers, far more soldiers would be deployed to the arctic, and not in the nice warm huts of the DEW line.

"What is the status report soldier?" asked the Captain leading the PPCLI patrol on Devon Island.

"We think this thing is not from here" replied a Ranger with the nickname of 'Moose' who had a worried look on his face and an unlit 'player's light' cigarette hanging from his mouth.

"What makes you say that?" Captain Logan inquired.

"Well, look at it. It isn't from around here. An elbow shaped plane? Who ever heard of that?" Replied another Ranger.

"True, but them commies are always experimenting with new designs"; was a statement heard coming from a PPCLI soldier standing in the group.

Captain Logan responded that they need to ascertain the origin of this plane first, before they could make any assumptions like that.

Captain Logan was a career soldier and all who met him could determine that right away. Although he was only 30, he had planned on a long career with the military. He was noticed and liked by his superiors and subordinates alike. He could realistically expect a good and long career. His subordinates respected him, and they always felt that he had their best interests in all situations. These were good skills for an officer to have. Even his own warrant officer on this particular mission could tease him while out of earshot of the other soldiers. Often his warrant officer would tell him that there is nothing in the world more dangerous that a captain with a map and compass. But Captain Logan would find ways to get back at him, of course this was done in fun with much respect.

Captain Logan got further information on what the Rangers had done and sensed there was something further that they hesitated to say. He asked; "Is this everything?"

The Ranger looked down for a moment then said; "not really, there is one other thing." He had a further delay before he continued to speak. "We saw a creature come out through a hatch that we can't see anymore. Look at this thing, there is no way in or out of it. We tried to enter the craft to search for survivors but could not find a hatch or doorway anywhere. We saw one from a distance, but once it closed, we couldn't even find the lines of the hatch. And the creature, it was very different".

"How so?" Captain Logan asked, now himself just a touch shaken up, yet trying not to show that to anyone.

"It had grayish skin, but it was hard to tell in this light, it was short, a small wide nose, but it had no nostrils. And no ears, not even holes for ears. But we only saw from a distance of maybe ten meters and with so little light but we did shine a flashlight on it. It had stood there and stared at us, and we had done the same. Maybe half a minute, and then it went up the stairs to the hatch and the hatch closed. We ran to where the hatch was and saw nothing, not even the seams of a hatch."

The PPCLI staff along with the Rangers put together the arctic tents and unloaded the remainder of the equipment from the pallets dropped by the CC130 Plane. The arctic tents resembled a small olive drab circus tent that slept about six people. A portable Harris high frequency (HF) radio was set up and in short time a complete bivouac site was in place. One member of the crew had always volunteered as the unit cook. He could start preparing meals while others had their duties to perform. Sure, in the morning the cook had to get up far earlier than the others, but he never drew fire picket (night watch shifts), so the trade-off was great for him. Besides, the others liked his cooking, so everyone was happy. Captain Logan really appreciated him as he contributed to the good morale of this unit. And good morale was critical at this time.

The entire time the site was being set up, there were always two members fully armed watching the craft. One was armed with a standard issue FN-C1A1, the other with an FN-C2A1 which was similar but included a bipod and was fully automatic. As there was still so much unknown, they had to assume the occupants were not friendly. By the second day, the infantry soldiers had assumed that the craft was not from Earth. This was based on the aircraft, and the description of the occupant given by the Rangers. This caused a level of fear that the Captain had never seen in his team before. He decided to double the number of staff guarding them while they did their research. Four soldiers would watch the craft while the others took photos, measured, and other chores around the location. All the soldiers carried their weapons at all times.

When they left Calgary, they had no idea what this craft was; it was assumed it could be Soviet or maybe even Chinese, so they came armed for a possible battle. They had four AN/PRC-25 set radios, 2FN-C2A1 rifles (Like the C1, but with a 30-round magazine, longer barrel, bipod, plus the ability to fire full auto), six sub machine guns (smg's), and the remainder were FN-C1A1 rifles. There was also an explosives kit used for breaching doors or other uses. There was an assortment of smoke canisters, and even a few grenades amongst their kit.

Captain Logan hoped deep down that they would not need this weaponry. In addition to not wanting a fight, he questioned if they had enough or powerful enough weapons to hold off this craft and those inside. He contemplated a radio call requesting both more equipment and possibly even more soldiers. He dismissed the idea after considering that it may result to unnecessary deaths of soldiers.

So, Captain Logan decided to have the soldiers watching the craft pull back another one hundred meters to watch. This gave them a bigger arc of cover and they could watch better as the others conducted measurements of the craft. But they all felt an intense uneasiness about this operation.

Chapter five

First Contact

After about one week of the arrival of the PPCLI, the captain could clearly see that his group were getting impatient. They had all finished their assigned tasks except the biggest one, entry into the craft. If it was a Soviet plane, which they had extreme doubts about, the occupants would need to come out sometime, and likely they would come out shooting. The captain had walked the length of the craft at least one hundred times in the preceding week. The lights had now all been turned off and there was not much sound coming from within the craft. With each walk of the length of the craft, he looked carefully for signs of an entrance point. He still never found one, which gave the Rangers description more credibility.

He could see that his crew was getting more and more uncomfortable with the passing each hour that nothing happened with the craft. Even the normally Jovial Rangers were still looking uncomfortable with the downed airplane near them. So, the captain thought they should take some of the C4 explosives and place it where the rangers had seen the hatch. Breaching the fuselage seemed like the only way they were ever going to gain entrance to the craft. They all felt this way, but respected Captain Logan's timing.

He called all the staff together and discussed the idea and asked for feedback on where they should place the C4, who was going to enter the craft, and who was going to provide cover. It was decided that the Rangers would stay back a distance with their Lee-Enfields, and the PPCLI would have six men enter. One soldier worked the explosives, and a field medic would stay outside ready to enter if needed. The remainder would be available if things went bad.

The captain had no problem finding volunteers for entry. Much to everyone's surprise, the soldier who was a self-professed field chef nicknamed 'Cook' was first to volunteer to enter the craft. Cook was actually keen on combat, but not interrupted sleep.

The demolition member approached the area where the hatch was believed to exist. He studied the metal siding for any hint of a seam or line where a door would be. He saw nothing but took a guess and packed a small ribbon of C4 around to create an opening. A detonator was placed in the C4 and wires were trailed out for some distance to a safe point. He pulled out the detonator and did a quick battery check. It had full power. He attached the wires to the detonator and turned on the unit to charge up the capacitor for the detonation.

"Fire in the hole, fire in the hole, fire in the hole" he yelled as he depressed the detonator button. Anticipating the blast and shock wave, he was kneeling with his head down. The entry team was a safe distance back but still close enough to make the short sprint to the entry point.

The blast never occurred, the wires were checked, the battery level was good, and the blasting cap was replaced for a new one in the rare event it was a dud. For a second time the explosives member yelled out "fire in the hole, fire in the hole, fire in the hole". The button was depressed again, but like the first time, nothing happened.

Just as the detonator was being re-examined, a hatch suddenly appeared and slowly opened. All the crew raised their rifles to the ready position, safeties are now off. A ramp slowly came down and after a moment seemingly appearing straight out of the craft itself. Then a small grayish human like body appeared wearing a reflective green padded suit. The creature was followed by four more of the same.

At least three of the soldiers started to panic at the sight of this creature. Clearly not of this world but another planet from who knows where. Those three placed their finger on the trigger and one by one started squeezing.

Somehow nothing happened from any of their rifles. Not a click, nothing. Later it was reported that none of them could move their trigger even a hair. It was as if the trigger was welded in place.

As the aliens exited the craft, the soldiers first noticed the height of them; they were short, being from just less than four feet tall to the tallest at about five feet tall (their height was determined later). The skin colour was very different too. It was light grey and at first, they appeared sickly. But it was just the normal colour for these creatures. They had thin bodies, and you could tell instinctively which ones were male and which ones were female; although there was little seen to make this conclusion obvious, such as breasts, but somehow you just knew which were male and which were female.

The cook, who was closest to the creature, felt the most unusual sensation. In his mind he heard the grey being speaking to him in perfect English. He felt the strongest sensation of peace and a euphoria that he had never felt before. He felt so secure in knowing they were not going to harm him. The words spoken to him were clearly that of begging them not to hurt them as they come in peace to study our planet. The cook believed them completely.

Not long after that, the Rangers also had the same experience; only to them the language was not English but Inuktitut. Later they would all discuss and compare their various experiences, but these were collectively what they experienced.

The Captain was next to experience this; he found that he could even speak back to them by his thoughts. The thought that the gray beings could be setting a trap had never crossed anyone's mind; clearly these beings projected a confidence in the minds of all of them. In addition to projecting words right into the brains of the soldiers, they could also project feelings into the minds of those who they are communicating with. Once again it never occurred to them how dangerous it could potentially be.

With the feeling of trust overwhelming them, the captain ordered all to lower their rifles which were done immediately. The first creature to emerge out of the hatch slowly walked towards the soldier who liked to cook and coincidently had the nickname of 'Cook'. He then heard in his head words clearly coming from the being.

The words "I like cooking too. But I don't know if we would like each other's food" was conveyed from the grey being directly to the mind of Cook. There was a sense by Cook that the being was teasing him about their tastes, but he didn't know. Nor did it immediately occur to Cook that this creature knew things about him that he had never said.

Cook thought to himself "how would we know if we wouldn't like each other's food unless we tried it?"

Much to Cooks' shock, the grey being responded directly to his thought. "I guess you are right, but the things we eat are likely very different. Perhaps we should try and find out?"

As Cook and this creature were having a telepathic conversation, more grey beings emerged from the hatch. One approached the captain and spoke to him in his head. "I am in charge of this craft and these are my crew. We crashed here and are trying to fix this so we can leave. But I am afraid it is much more serious that we had thought at first. It is clearly beyond our ability to repair this craft."

The Captain thought about how a craft as amazing as this that could travel from other stars or maybe even other galaxies could possibly crash here. Just as he completed this thought in his mind, a reply came back to him nearly instantly.

"We were flying about six kilometers above the ice when we noticed that we were going to collide with one of your craft (likely the Boeing 707 Captain Logan heard about from his briefing). We took evasive action to avoid hitting it when our equipment misread the gravity of your planet and reset. We could not recover in time and crash landed here. The very gravity of your planet could not be calculated by our machinery in time to recover, so we crashed here due to the fault of one simple machine, but the crash caused other failures that we do not believe we can fix. In addition, we have several injured on-board our vessel. Our craft was severely mangled, but we build it from memory metal, and it regained its shape within minutes of the crash. Sadly, some of the occupants inside didn`t do so well.

All the Rangers and PPCLI members in attendance felt a level of comfort with these creatures, and a level of compassion due to their unfortunate circumstances. In the after-action-report (AAR) it was noted that each and every one of them knew without any doubt that they were safe with these aliens. There was no fear of them, but there was an intense feeling that the aliens should be helped by the soldiers in fixing their craft and especially looking after the wounded ones.

Cook was invited inside by the alien he was conversing with. But at that point the Corporal stepped towards him and ordered him to stay.

The order came not as a fear of intent of the aliens, but out of concern for a debriefing meeting and the reporting to occur first. Medical supplies were needed, and assessments needed to be conducted.

The captain sent his two medics to find out the number of injuries and conditions of them for treatment, but without entering the craft. It was determined that there were six creatures injured, and twenty-four uninjured or with only minor injuries. Thirty-two aliens in total were on the craft. Plus, there were a couple who had succumbed to their injuries in the crash. The captain ordered that all cloth bandages, splints and supplies that did not include medications be provided to them. The use of medications was denied for fear that the effects on these beings could be unpredictable due to different body chemistry. The medical staff of these creatures seemed to understand that.

Once the medical supplies were handed over to them, the captain excused himself to go contact NDHQ (National Defence Headquarters) on the Harris Teletype set. Some members of the alien craft advised that they are going to re-enter their ship for rest, yet others remained outside with the soldiers, despite the very cold temperatures.

After Captain Logan made the walk back to the camp, the captain entered his arctic tent and proceeded to the radio set. Using the encrypted teletype machine, he typed out his report and sent it off with the simple push of the transmit button. Usually it took a few hours for follow-up instructions to be returned, but to his shock, the teletype machine started printing out the reply within a few minutes.

> Are you sure that the creatures are not a threat or are not aggressive? Please detail your answer. What supplies are needed and why? How long do they intend to stay? Instruct all staff that this is now the highest level of secrecy and they are not to discuss it.

Captain Logan walked approximately two kilometers back to the craft. During that walk he reflected on what he had to ask the aliens, but more importantly he was questioning in his own mind if this was real. He now had a fear of them come over himself. Captain Logan realised that the feeling of peace must have been projected into his mind by them. What other feelings could they project? Was this a ploy to take them all off guard? Clearly all the infantry soldiers and Canadian Rangers there were under mind control too. The more Captain Logan thought about this, the more he worried that his men, his country and possibly his planet might be in some real serious trouble. Now he was feeling sick to his stomach as he thought about the possibilities.

As he approached the craft, he could sense the feelings of peace overcome him again, but he kept his concerns active in his brain realizing that these thoughts are probably projected from the aliens. It was a weird mix of emotions, peace and being comforted, yet trying to remain scared and confused as he knew he should be. Mix in with this the feeling of helplessness and intense stress, and Captain Logan felt nausea slowly creep up on him.

Just as he was approaching the remaining space craft crew, the one who telepathically explained to him how the craft crashed, approached him for more dialogue.

The thought came into Captain Logan's mind; "I know you are feeling sick due to the confusion you have. You show good qualities being concerned for not only your staff, but your land as well. I know that we have not earned your trust yet, and I accept this as time will show you the truth. Yes, it is true we put the feelings of peace into your minds, but we didn't do this for any reason other than to build a foundation with you. It was never our intent to be deceptive. I will instruct my crew to cease this at once so that you know we are not trying to be controlling".

Captain Logan replied by thought; "No, don`t do that yet. When I have all my people back at our bivouac site, I will tell them then and you can cease projecting that feeling after we have left here for the evening. Otherwise you might cause panic with them".

"Agreed;" Replied the alien, himself appearing relieved.

"Cook, on me now" ordered Captain Logan.

"Sir" came the immediate reply as he double time approached the captain.

"Please return to the bivouac site and start preparing the dinner. I will have the remaining staff leave here in one hour. Please make it a good meal; I think the group will need it."

"Sir, with pleasure;" came the response. Cook, of all people understood the importance of food when it came to good morale. There is an old saying in the military that the two most important people for morale are the cook and the payroll staff. The other saying that often crossed the minds of soldiers is that an army marches on their stomachs. Both statements are very true.

Cook immediately headed off to the bivouac site to start preparing supper for the crew. It was reported later in his after-action report that as he got further away from the craft, he too felt fear overcome him from the aliens. The feeling of being incredibly unsafe overcame him too. He found himself constantly looking over his shoulder back at the craft to see if everything was alright, but the distance was too great to really see anything.

Cook got to the POL pit. The POL pit stood for 'Petroleum, Oil and Lubricants' which were always stored a safe distance from tents. There he filled the Coleman stove with naphtha for the evening ahead. He also filled up the lanterns to have light inside the tent. He hung the lanterns in the tent and looked through the food supplies for ideas for a meal.

Cook, decided to prepare the remainder of the fresh rations which consisted of some mystery meat he could kind of pass off as steak. With it he prepared rice that soldiers often complained "didn't taste as good as the box that it came in". But cook loved to open up the ration packs and pilfer items to make the fresh food taste better. Last was cans of green beans. Just as the meal was about ready to be served, Captain Logan and the other PPCLI crew, along with the Canadian Rangers showed up for dinner and the Captains briefing.

"Listen up people." barked Captain Logan. His crew from Calgary appreciated and respected him. The intuit crew from the Canadian Rangers were quickly learning that he could be trusted and had their best intentions in mind always. "Today is a monumental day, we met with and communicated with aliens" As the captain looked around the modular tent, he could see the expressions on their faces of fear. He didn't see those expressions when they were over two kilometers away at the craft, but he sure saw them now.

"I had a conversation with their CO" (Commanding officer). "It seems that they have the capability to remove fear from our minds, and that is what they had done when we were there. Now that you are back in the bivouac site that normal fear has returned. I expressed my concern that it could be perceived as fraudulent by us, and he was prepared to stop that immediately. I suggested that he wait until we have left for the evening. I expressed my concern about not understanding their intentions in light of the false feelings. I was assured that it was for no purpose other than to establish contact with us. The question now is do we trust them?"

There was some muttering amongst the soldiers that Captain Logan had allowed to continue for a couple minutes before getting their attention again. It seemed that some others had also come to the realization of the projected feelings.

"So, we are going to have to be cautious. We are going to observe carefully. We are going to trust as best as we can. But we will not be pushed; nor will we assume we are safe with them. We will be cautious at all times." Captain Logan let these words hang for a moment before asking "are then any questions at this point?"

One of the soldiers, the warrant officer asked about aggression on behalf of the soldiers. Captain Logan was certain that the question was more aimed as a statement towards the Ranges as opposed to directing it at the PPCLI staff. But the Captain knew what he was getting at and wanted to keep things equal between his men and the Rangers. So, he replied to all to be extra careful not to show any aggression as they did not know how the aliens would respond.

The Canadian Rangers were used to this from regular members of the military. Often the regulars would look down on these volunteers. But these volunteers knew that they would in time prove themselves worthy of all respect. They were hard workers and knew this land better than anyone else. Even if they were not that familiar with Devon Island, they knew about arctic survival. Most Inuit avoided this island as it was an arctic desert. You actually need snow as an insulator in these temperatures. Frostbite on their feet was a real concern.

Captain Logan had taken the opportunity to address everyone in the bivouac site about how to behave with the aliens. "If we were conducting a rescue operation in a foreign country, we would be cautious but helpful. We would trust until given a reason not to. At this point we are on a rescue mission, let's keep that in mind. So, with this in mind, what equipment do we need?"

"We need tools." Spoke a voice from the rear.

Another yelled out, "Aircraft mechanics."

Still another suggested a modular tent with an immersion heater as well as tables and chairs.

After some general discussion about the required equipment to be air dropped, Cook finally spoke up with a question. "How long do we think it will take?"

"What are you getting at Cook?" asked the Captain.

"Well, in April the sun will start to come out. A month or so later and it will be daylight around the clock. When the Russians do their flyovers, they are going to see this. What are we going to do about that? Their reconnaissance planes will pick it up in no time. And worse, what if they think it is a new long-range bomber of ours or the Americans, and they decide to bomb it before it can be used. We will all be killed.

"I hadn't thought about that." Replied Captain Logan. "You pose a great question and a really good concern, anyone have any ideas?"

"How about camouflage tarps like tanks use?" came another random voice.

"How are we supposed to work on the craft when there is a tarp over it?" Replied someone else.

A Canadian Ranger yelled out; "why not use the modular tents like we usually use? They can be linked together indefinitely."

Captain Logan suggested that although they could be linked to form an endless tent, the width was nowhere near wide enough nor was it tall enough to cover this craft. Still, he liked the brainstorming of ideas, and just as important, he liked seeing the regular members working with the volunteers. Not long after this discussion, the briefing was adjourned so that they could get some much-needed rest.

Captain Logan returned to the teletype set of the Harris radio. He proceeded to type in all the equipment they would need. This included an aircraft mechanic as well as other technical experts. In addition, he explained the concern of daylight a few months away and the idea of custom modular tent.

This time Captain Logan did not get a quick reply. In fact, it was not until after breakfast the next day. The teletype machine had a paper waiting in the tray to read. They wanted the full dimensions for a custom-made tent, especially the height and width. Captain Logan realised that the cost of this custom equipment must be very expensive, so obviously this was a much bigger concern than he thought. He reviewed the notes on dimensions and quickly entered in the required numbers into the Harris set.

Chapter Six

I would like to buy a tent

Down south in Vancouver it was a typical overcast day of almost 12 degrees on October 14th, 1966. Jones Tent and Awning was a manufacturing company based in Vancouver located in the community of Kitsilano for many years and had a reputation for durable well-made products. Their products were known world-wide. The famous 'Trapper Nelson' backpack was made by this company. They worked with heavy canvas when producing industrial strength tents, awnings or other canvas products for businesses or individual use.

This company was very used to custom orders, this making up a good part of their business. They had a history of some military contracts as well. The custom work they did varied from whether it was an awning for a store front or someone's home, or custom tents for a children's summer camp, or an industrial logging camp. Their products were top notch and they took pride in their workmanship and materials.

Although Jones Tent and Awning did have a store front, they rarely had walk in customers for unique and very big orders, but this day was to be very different for this company. Two senior officers based in the Jericho Bivouac at Point Grey in Vancouver's West side entered the building and approached the sales staff requesting an immediate meeting with their sales manager. The clerk behind the counter observed their uniforms and felt this was a priority, so he went immediately to get the sales manager.

After a couple minutes, the sales manager came out to greet the soldiers. He was a short stocky man who clearly enjoyed his Job. "Good morning. My name is David, how can I be of assistance to you?"

The first officer replied; "Is there somewhere we can talk in private please?"

David sensed the urgency of their request for privacy and quickly directed them to his office. "Right this way;" replied David. "We can use my office in the back." David led them out back of the store and through an area used for both storage and manufacturing. There were huge bolts of canvas stacked neatly in piles. In the center of the room was tables used for cutting and measuring the canvas. They proceeded through this large room until the three entered a small office that had just enough seating for all of them. It was clearly an office used for work and not for meeting with customers, the desk was piled high with papers, and bookshelves had an overflow of swatches of different thicknesses of canvas and of course the different colours available too. "Sorry for the mess, I don't usually have customers visiting my office."

The first officer said; "Please do not concern yourself about the clutter in your office. You obviously work hard. And please allow me to make introductions. I am Lieutenant Colonel Barrett and with me is

Major French. Thank you for taking some time to see us, especially without us making an appointment".

"It is my pleasure, we here at Jones Tent and Awning have produced goods for the military before and is always willing to do what we can for you."

"That is excellent. Well, we have a rather unique and rush order for you. It is an exceptionally large modular tent. We are wondering if it can be made and if it can be made on time? And, I am afraid that there isn't that much time available to you." Commented Major French.

"Let see what you need done. We are known for making the occasional miracle happen." Replied David with a hint of pride in his voice. It was clear to the soldiers that David was proud of the work he did and wanted Jones Tent and Awning to be the best company for their products.

Lt. Col Barrett produced a document that showed the specifications for the custom modular tent. It needed to be twelve meters tall in the center, sloping to seven meters tall in the sides before going almost straight down to the ground. The length of each section from front to back needed to be thirty meters so that the width of the assembled tent was that wide, but in the center where the craft took a near ninety-degree bend, it was approaching nearly fifty meters wide. To make things really difficult, there could be no vertical support poles except at the sides. Also, it needed a high wind rating. Fortunately, due to Devon Island being an arctic desert, there was little concern about rain and minimal snow build up. The only snow they would see would be brought in by wind from other ground locations, so it would simply blow off the tent too. This did make the canvas much lighter to work with. And as rain was not really an issue, the seams were easier to make and there was no need for water-proofing which also served to keep the weight down. Wind was their only concern.

David reviewed the order and looked up to see if they were joking about this order. Even for a large company like Jones Tent and Awning, this was an engineering concern of monumental proportions, and the manufacturing costs would be staggering.

"This is more like a circus tent." Replied David in a stressed-out tone. "We would need to hire a structural engineer for consultation purposes for the metal support system. In addition, we would have to compensate staff for all the overtime if it is truly a rush order. Also due to the size, we will have to contract out the manufacturing of the metal supports. Our tent poles here just won't do."

"So, I am giving you the authorization to do just that" Replied the Lieutenant Colonel.

David looked puzzled and replied, "You don't want a quote first? I didn't think the military could buy a thumb tack without a quote. We could get that for you within the week."

"Honestly, you will need to start working on this immediately. You have provided government contracts before. We know we can trust you. Especially if you wish to have future contracts too." Replied Major Dixon in a half joking manor. "Also, if we wait for the quote, that would significantly cut down the time you have for production of this tent. Best you just start on it right away and we can forward a retainer immediately to assist in covering your manufacturing expenses."

"Thank you for putting your trust in our company. When do you need this by?" Replied David, now realizing how serious these two were about this order.

"You have eight weeks from today to complete the order. You had best look for that engineer right away." Said Major Dixon.

"With eight weeks, I can say without a doubt that we will require our staff to work considerable overtime. I will ensure detailed logs of all expenses are provided"

"Thank you." The Lt Col then concluded by saying that "this order will not be discussed with anyone except the design team. As far as the assembly crew are concerned, it is simply bigger pieces sewn together. They have no need to understand the assembled size."

"But the engineer will need to know more than that, in order for him do his Job properly."

"True, but only for each section. The full details about the overall length will be left out for the engineer; he only needs the specifications for each section of the modular tent." Spoke Lt. Col. Brad. "And he does not need to know who this contract is for."

"I understand. I will have the design team start on it immediately" Replied David. David looked both excited to have such a big order as well as scared that he has taken on a project that was too big for him to handle.

Lt. Col Barrett and Major French left the shop and proceeded towards the staff car parked next to the Carling O'Keefe's Brewery. Major French spoke first. "Do you think David is as confused about it as we are?"

Lt. Col Barrett replied; "I would give my left arm to know why we had to order this tent. This is so strange a design."

"Sir, I think we will never know."

Chapter Seven

More equipment please

Back on Devon Island, on morning of October 15th, breakfast was served by Cook. All enjoyed the scrambled powdered eggs, something that remotely resembled toast, and coffee that was nice and hot, but that was about it. Captain Logan walked over to the Harris set and retrieved the teletype paper.

It read as follows;

Your request for the sectional tent to cover the craft has been approved and a company will be contacted today for manufacture to the specifications required on an expedited basis. Anticipated delivery will be eight to ten weeks maximum. In addition, your request for tools including a large generator, lighting, air compressor, and others will also be approved. Expect delivery in two days by air drop, weather permitting. As for the request for aircraft mechanics, and other specialists, this request is denied. You will commence the work yourselves to the best of your skills and abilities. There will be no further staff or relief staff sent to your location for the duration of this mission.

The Captain read that three times before calling his staff to pay attention to his announcement. "Listen up people, we are getting the tent the Rangers have suggested, we are getting all the tools you identified, but here is the kicker; you are now all aircraft mechanics. We will not have any help arriving at all. We are on our own and will likely be here for some time without replacements. All the equipment we requested, besides the tent, arrives in two days by air drop. So, until then, let's go to the craft and get to know our guests better, and work on accomplishing our tasks. Now one other thing, as we are going to be here a very long time. If there are items that I can request to make us more comfortable, and our long stay more enjoyable, please let me know. I have no idea if it will be approved, but please ask me and I will put it forward. The worst thing that can happen is they say no to our request."

Captain Logan was a people person. He cared deeply for his subordinates and his subordinates trusted him and liked him right back. He could read them well too. He could see the fear in their eyes. He could see the uncertainty they have of the aliens. He could also see that they questioned what if the alien's intent is different from what they say it is. Also, they all wondered how long would they be stuck on Devon Island? The was still a feeling of disbelief that even Captain Logan had in common with them, although he kept this feeling to himself so not to cause further concerns or stress to his staff. The uncertainty of their situation clearly scared most, if not all of them. They could train for combat, they could train for search and rescue operations, and they could train for all-out war. But not one of them had ever trained for contact with aliens. And none of them had any more than rudimentary knowledge of mechanics. But yet here they were, by circumstance now thrown into a situation way above their training, and highest level of security a soldier could ever face. The military didn't even have the luxury of a screening by military police or the intelligence section. So, they knew that things must be very serious in order for the military to place them in this situation. Captain Logan would be giving briefings to them in the coming weeks and months about the seriousness of keeping this project to themselves.

After Breakfast, the Warrant Officer wisely ordered a general cleanup of the bivouac site. He believed that an orderly and clean bivouac would help to restore a sense of normal routine to the group. Also, it has always been the protocol for the military to do routine and regular cleanings of their site. This helped in moral by not having garbage lying around. Bags of garbage would be picked up by outgoing aircraft at a later time. When the day came that they were to leave, there would be no visible sign that they were ever there to begin with.

Once the camp was ready to pass the Warrant Officers' inspection, they marched to the craft, a good half hour walk on a rocky covered ground. Of course, the standing joke in the military is that no section that is 'inspection ready' could ever pass a warrant officers inspection. This time the Warrant Officer and Captain told them to just walk there as a group. This allowed for a more casual approach to hopefully set a better mood. As they approached the ground, they were met by the alien crew. Fear overcame all the Canadian soldiers, but they could also see that the aliens too were afraid of them as well. In fact, Captain Logan felt that they may even have more fear as they clearly were stuck on a foreign planet where they were forced to trust in beings they knew nothing about. Captain Logan decided then and there that he would not violate their trust at all. He would always be honest and try his best to accommodate them. He and his soldiers were all the aliens had. And the aliens all knew it too. Without Captain Logan and his soldiers, the aliens would eventually die. Captain Logan was not going to let this happen.

The cook was the first of the soldiers to be approached by the aliens on this particular day. It was the same alien as he had talked to the day before. The alien who cooks for them spoke to Cook's mind and said, "Would you like a tour of our craft and the kitchen now?"

Captain Logan received that message in his brain too. He replied to Cook, "Go for the tour Cook; I would love to hear about what you see in their kitchen later." But Captain Logan directed Cook to leave his rifle outside the craft with another soldier. This worried Cook, but he complied anyway.

So, Cook left with the alien albeit scared and somewhat reluctantly. But he could also see that the alien cook was also very scared. Likely the alien cook was instructed much the same as him to try and get to know each other. Cook walked up to gangway to the hatch, it was a small hatch for Cook's larger size, but still he could get in ducking only a small amount. Once inside, he learned that he was just tall enough to walk upright without ducking his head. He was just shy of six feet tall, so he estimated the height of the ceiling to be about six feet two inches.

The first thing Cook had noticed was the lighting and warmth he felt while in the craft. The lights were bright, but not too bright, and the temperature felt just right to Cook. Cook was led down a long hallway that contained many doors off to other directions. The doors somewhat reminded him of doors on a submarine, yet he had never actually been on one, he only saw them in movies. They entered one door where Cook had to slightly duck his head as not to hit it in the doorway. Once inside he quickly saw that it was the food stores and supply room. He could see banks and banks of shelving that looked like it was polished stainless steel. Each shelf appeared to have a locking arm to hold all the containers in place without movement. Clearly all the food containers were identical but Cook guessed that the contents were very different. The writing on each shelf and container roughly resembled Hebrew characters. Obviously, this was the aliens' written language, but it could have also been Sanskrit for all that Cook knew.

The alien clearly heard Cooks thoughts and pointed out that they all held mostly the same foods as their diet did not vary much. Cook asked him how he liked that as humans loved different flavours and varieties plus, we got bored easily with the same foods.

The alien replied that this was not a problem for them as their bodies liked the nutritional content more than the taste.

Cook also asked the Alien how long this could feed the crew for. The Alien replied that it would last their entire crew the equivalent of nearly six earth years with what they had left on board this craft.

Finally Cook asked his host what his name is. He figured if he is going to be stuck on Devon Island for however long it will be, he should at least start to learn the names of these aliens.

The alien replied a name that sounded like Pench. For the first time since that day started, they both felt a little more comfortable with each other. Still a long way to go before either could relax. Pench asked Cook what his name was.

"My name is Steven Jones, but everyone here just calls me Cook, as I always seem to be the one who cooks the meals" Cook replied. Then Cook told Pench his theory about how volunteering for always being the cook had got him out of doing many of the other less desirable tasks. Pench seemed to enjoy this explanation of his reasons for doing the cooking. "I can even get out of doing the dishes too." He bragged to Pench. Pench appeared to be very amused by this story. Cook started to think to himself that Pench was female, something he didn't notice at first as the Aliens bodies were less obvious of their gender than humans were.

It was as if Pench understood Cook, because the thought that entered his mind was first a little embarrassment, followed by the words in his mind; "Yes I am a female."

Cook noticed a smile on Penchs' face and he was smiling back.

The tour that Cook went on had continued back into the hallway, where he could see the others from his camp being given one on one tours of the craft as well. Each one of the tours seemed to be conducted by someone of their similar specialties. The captain of the soldier's group was with the alien captain, and the medic was getting a tour of the sick bay by an alien Cook had assumed was their medic.

Cook then entered the galley to see what looked more like a modern morgue that anyplace he had ever seen to prepare food. Pench must have read his thoughts because for the first time Cook heard a noise come from an Alien. Obviously Pench thought this was funny and was trying to suppress a laugh. Cook was a little embarrassed by this, but he also didn't want to insult the alien. Suddenly they both laughed together.

Meanwhile, Captain Logan was visiting the bridge with the alien officer in charge. The captain also inquired about the alien's name. The captain learned that the Alien was called Scara.

"How long have you commanded this group?" Inquired Scara.

"Only about six months. I joined the military about six years ago, right after finishing University." Replied Captain Logan. "I would like to ask you the same question"

"When I was young, I worked on a cargo spacecraft in the bridge as a junior navigator. I would have been the equivalent age of seventeen earth years old. I worked about twenty-five of your years slowly gaining more experience and taking courses along the way. About eight years ago I qualified to be a captain of a spacecraft." Scara said with a hint of pride but no arrogance.

It was obvious to Captain Logan that Scara was proud of his staff, and proud of his own accomplishments, but not in an arrogant way. Despite this situation, he still presented himself as upbeat, yet Captain Logan suspected that he was feeling depressed.

Scara read his thoughts. "It's not that I am feeling like I let my crew down, this was a malfunction of the brain of this ship that let us down. I am sad for my crew who will likely never see their friends and family again. Sure, they all knew the risks when we left for this voyage, but we hope those situations never occur. So, I am sad for my crew".

"What about yourself?"

"What about me? My life has been around craft as long as I know it. I have no family, but of course I will still miss my home planet. But as I have spent my life traveling the galaxy, I have spent less than thirty percent of my entire life on my home planet. So, for me my home is on this craft or others".

Scara and Captain Logan were deep in conversation while Scara conducted a tour of the craft. Particular attention was given to the bridge and to the workings of the craft.

Scara showed real enthusiasm when giving Captain Logan the bridge tour. He showed the various controls, and all the different places for staff to sit. The captain was surprised to learn that all the engineering work was done from the bridge and not from the engine room. That was when Scar told him in his head that there is not a proper engine room, but twenty compartments that led by conduit to a larger electrical compartment. But there is little room for staff inside there.

Captain Logan asked about the many features of the craft, but sadly could not understand much of what has been told to him by Scara. The technical details were more than Captain Logan could understand. Even the explanation of how to steer this vessel went above Captain Logan's comprehension.

Scara then looked a little sad and Logan learned that there was a real concern that the craft could never be fixed. Captain Logan tried to sound upbeat and assure him that it could and that he and his government would do everything they can to fix this craft and allow them to leave here. Still Scara looked downhearted.

Captain Logan could clearly see there was little he could do to convince Scara that they could help. Scara then led him to one of the many small electrical engine compartments to point out the problem. Sadly, Captain Logan had no idea what he was looking at. Scara pointed at the issue as if it should be clear as the nose on Captain Logan's face, but he still had no idea what he was looking at. He was told it was the brain of the ship, but to Captain Logan it could have been a coffee percolator for all he knew. But Captain Logan did sense that Scaras' fear of being stuck on earth was not unfounded. These thoughts made Captain Logan feel sadness too.

If you can tell me what you need to fix this, I will get my government to obtain it and air-drop it here for you. Scara assured him that the technology here on Earth is not advanced enough to either replace broken parts or to even repair them. Deep down Captain Logan knew Scara was right, although he asked anyway. There was a mutual sadness felt over the thoughts of this. They continued on with the tour. In addition, Captain Logan was not even sure that the government would assist them, not without something being offered to make it worthwhile.

Scara could read the thoughts of Captain Logan and hear that he was wondering how this craft worked. So Scara began to telepathically tell him.

"We work with gravity to make this craft move." Replied Scara

"Wouldn't it only be able to fall down?"

"In a sense, yes it would. But what if you could change were down is? We can. We can even do that here on your planet. We create an area in front of the craft that has extreme gravity; therefore, the craft always falls towards that area. Even if here on your planet we create that area above us. We literally fall up, instead of down. Instead of what you would call an engine that pushes a craft, we create a field of high gravity area in front of the craft and constantly fall in the direction of our travel."

"But couldn't you only reach terminal velocity?" Captain Logan inquired after remembering his high school physics class from over ten years before.

"You are thinking of Earth's gravity, not what gravity could be in other places, or here under different circumstances."

"That sounds like it would be inefficient? Doesn't it use extreme amounts of power?" Captain Logan inquired.

"Far less than you would imagine, especially in space. Once we are going, we need very little power to continue in the same direction. We use more here on your planet, but still it uses far less power than anything you have here."

"What do you use to power this craft?" Inquired Captain Logan

"We utilize a highly radioactive element that you do not have. We can get so much energy from only a small amount, and that can fly this craft for years of your time."

Scara continued on the tour with Captain Logan, showing him everything from his private quarters to the mess hall. Despite the large size of the craft, the entire tour would have been relatively short had it not been for the conversations along the way. Scara and Captain Logan were feeling a trust for one another. Scara had no choice but to trust, knowing they would be there for the remainder of their lives. Captain Logan knew that too, so his fear was subsiding, despite questioning if it would be possible that they could still get the craft fixed. Captain Logan thought he was questioning it only out of a sense of optimism. Clearly, he felt compassion towards these aliens.

On another part of the craft, the Master Corporal who acted as the PPCLI's medic was getting a tour of the sick bay. This soldier was affectionately called 'Doc' by his team. It rapidly became clear to him that his host knew far more about patching up the wounded then he would ever hope to know. Also, he noticed several chamber-like beds with other aliens in them. He walked up to them to look inside. Some appeared asleep or dead, but with that thought, the alien immediately implanted the feeling in his head that they are all alive, but sadly not all of them would likely live much longer. Some of them had injuries that they would certainly recover from, as they were simple broken bones sustained from the crash. The alert aliens looked back at him through the glass of their chambers. Doc felt sadness for them all. It was an empathy he never knew he had. His training told him to not think about the welfare of his patients, but to just treat the injury, and worry about them later after the danger had passed. This was done so his feelings would not get in the way of his work. But here, Doc could not help but feel a sense of deep compassion and a strong worry for them. He was not used to this feeling of empathy for them. The team arrived at Devon Island with the thoughts that they may be rescuing a downed aircraft. He had narcotics, antibiotics, and IV solutions back at the camp. He wanted to use them so bad, but he knew that Captain Logan was right. They didn't know how the alien bodies would handle their medications. It was best not to use them.

Through his thoughts, Doc asked the alien medic what supplies the injured needed for their recovery. The alien replied that he was scared to use our medicines too, as he had no idea how they would work on his injured. But he did ask for antiseptic solutions as well as a narcotic pain killer to test on the most critically wounded alien. In addition, splints and bandages would always be useful.

Later once the tours with all the staff was concluded, the soldiers returned to the bivouac site for lunch and discussions about what each had seen.

Captain Logan conducted another short briefing to learn what new requests they had. He was going to put in a new list for supplies to be added to the next air drop.

Everyone agreed that despite feeling fear from the aliens and especially while inside their craft, they all felt a little better, and the aliens treated them all very respectfully. One of the soldiers gave some interesting news that Captain Logan didn't know. The aliens were not soldiers, they were not even scientists as such (although there were some scientists on their craft), nor were they even some sort of other worldly ambassadors. The closest titled you could give them was an alien version of what earthlings would call missionaries here to see if humans would be receptive to them.

Of course, these aliens were not interesting in telling us about their God, but they want to help us be a better planet. Captain Logan knew this information would need to go into his report to NDHQ (National Defence Headquarters) in Ottawa. He wondered how the staff reading his report would respond when learning this information.

Captain Logan went to the Teletype machine to work on an update to send off. A few minutes later he returned to the mess to socialise with his crew and the members from the Canadian Rangers who by now were considered part of the gang by the PPCLI group. They were all coming together as a team. This made Captain Logan very happy. It spoke volumes for all the subordinates under his charge.

Captain Logan's first priority is always the safety of his men; after that, the success of the mission became his next priority. So, the team of professional soldiers working alongside the volunteers, coming together as a tight knit group helped in the overall mission. Of course, a good officer puts his crew ahead of himself. Captain Logan had the respect of his group. They knew he would always go to bat for them. He also gave them all the credit for the teams' successes, and when there were any failures or shortcomings, he took all the responsibility. That is why his crew were so devoted to working with him.

But it went both ways, Captain Logan knew he could trust his men with his life. He knew their strengths and their limitations. And he was now figuring out the men in the Rangers. He could see that although they had their own culture, and an almost whimsical outlook, they were highly reliable too. They tried hard to appear laid back, almost lazy, but that was more of a persona that they often portrayed. They were smart and they were hard workers despite the laid-back attitude. They took their Job very seriously, and they understood the importance of the tasks. He could see that when they were in bivouac, they loved hearing about life in the big cities, but just as importantly, they were telling about life in the arctic and his men enjoyed these stories just as much. He also knew he could learn so much from them. Captain Logan quickly developed a deep respect for them that he knew his men from PPCLI were developing too.

The only thing that Captain Logan noticed that bothered him was the fact that as an avid non-smoker, these Rangers were smoking at almost every opportunity. He did not like the smell of cigarettes, but he also knew that if they smoke, then running out is not a good thing. He made a note to himself that the next supply order he had best include a few cartons of Players Light, as that seemed to be their cigarette of choice. Only a few of his men smoked and Captain Logan preferred it that way.

A soldier walked past the Harris Teletype machine which revealed another page had been received. It was retrieved and handed over to the Captain and read immediately.

"We have an air drop tonight at about three in the morning. We will need to set up flares for the touch and go. We need to ensure that an appropriate path is created without large boulders in the way. That will be our task the remainder of the day and likely well into the evening."

Despite the upcoming task to be carried out in dark and the bitter cold, they were all in a good mood knowing that they would get new supplies as well as some comforts to make their stay more enjoyable.

The sections warrant officer had wasted no time in getting the group to scout the area for the best direction of the airstrip. They were unsure if the plane would actually land, or just fly mere feet above the ground and drop the supplies out the back. In either case, they needed to be ready. Fortunately, the land near their camp was fairly level, and this made the task of where to put the makeshift runway much easier. The only real concern was the boulders scattered around the ground for some distance around their camp.

As it was permanently night time for several more months, this was all done in the dark. But after an hour of walking they came to a decision on the direction of the airstrip. The group formed an extended line and began passing the larger rocks down to the sides. After about four passes of the entire airstrip, Cook left the group to go back to bivouac to figure out a meal to prepare. Currently they were out of fresh rations, so whatever he made would come from cans or boxes. This was less enjoyable, but they all knew that Cook could only work with the items on hand. That would change as soon as the airdrop occurred.

After about one hour, the group came back from the makeshift airstrip for the meal that Cook had attempted to put together. Sadly, with nothing but canned goods left, there was little he could do to make it more palatable.

While they were eating, Captain Logan consulted the warrant officer to get a report on how the airstrip is progressing.

"There are just a few more big boulders that we will have to roll out of the way. It will take a few hands to do this as they are big. But after the meal, I am sure they will have some restored energy. But it is really cold out, I am glad the ground is very bare." Replied the warrant officer. "Can we get a weather report?"

"Actually, I can tell you the weather report now. Here on Devon Island it could almost be classified as a dessert. There is very little precipitation. As you can see, it is also a large bowl-shaped island so along the sides the wind is minimal. But it is cold. Currently it is minus 30 centigrade, but as the sun is down, over the coming weeks it will likely hit fifty below. I have requested modular tents, immersion heaters for the camp, and in addition to that, we will need strings of lights, diesel fuel, and we are running low on batteries for the flashlights. Also, the naphtha supply is getting lower too."

"Is all of this due to arrive in the early morning?"

"It is supposed to. What do you think we should ask for in the next load to keep morale going strong?"

"Beer sir"

"In this cold climate?"

"Once the immersion heaters are set up, we will be toasty warm here. And beer will be a good treat for the men. Perhaps some bags of potato chips and other snacks."

Captain Logan appreciated his Warrant Officer for thinking about the morale of his men too. As he thought about it, he came to realize that he was right about ordering in beer. He made notes in his notebook of these items.

Neither the warrant officer, nor the captain had noticed that the men from the Canadian Rangers had one by one got up from their meal and left the tent. Most of the men had laid down for a short rest before returning to the task of moving the boulders. About an hour later, the warrant officer instructed them to get up so the task could be finished. They figured that the Canadian Rangers had left the tent, but that they were simply outside for them to smoke.

Once outside, they could not spot the Rangers, and the Warrant officer was a little upset at them for skipping out on the final phase of their tasking. The remaining group started off towards the makeshift strip when they noticed faint lights from that area. When they got there, it became instantly obvious where the Rangers were. They had taken it upon themselves to clear the remaining large boulders. Still there were a couple huge ones that needed to be done. He could see that their flashlights batteries were nearly dead. There was a look of happiness and relief on the faces of the PPCLI soldiers as they came to realise that the bulk of this task was done for them by these rangers.

The captain was very proud of these Rangers too; they were selfless and hard working. He was certain to put this in his report as he wanted NDHQ to know about them too. The volunteers showed that they are strong workers, team players and great for morale. The two large remaining stones were quickly moved away when as many PPCLI soldiers, along with the Rangers, could get behind the rocks. The work almost resembled a team of players enjoying a sport. They all seemed to be happy with their successes. Also, now due to the Rangers, they all had some free time to enjoy. Free time is something that in the military doesn't happen too often. When it does happen, they all take advantage of it.

Back in bivouac, the group were sitting on their sleeping bags, talking and joking. Some were playing cards. One of the Rangers had a small board game called 'Arctic Hunt', which was a version of tic-tac-toe and was showing a regular member how to play.

Although there was a jovial mood in the modular tent shared by all, there was also the underlying fear of the unknown. Today's earlier meeting with the aliens was friendly and beneficial, but there was still a lack of trust that lent itself to fear of the unknown. Captain Logan talked with the crew openly to see where the concerns were. Was there something he could settle or fix to help build this trust? But in the end, it seemed that all the crew really needed was to talk it out. Trust needed to be built, but they did move much closer to that goal with the meetings they had that morning.

Over the next hour or so, the team started to settle in for some much-needed rest. Contrary to their normal routine, only one person remained up for fire picket and to ensure the camp is safe. There was little in the way of wildlife, and the threat of people at this remote location was minimal. Still, being that the cold war with the Soviet Union was going strong, the lone person on fire picket kept a watchful eye out for anything unusual.

At about two in the morning, they all got up and started their walk to the make-shift airstrip. Once there, each member was given two flares that resembled a standard automotive road flare. The crew was split in half with one half of them on one side of the runway, and the other half on the other. They then spaced themselves along the runway at equal distances on each side and waited for the plain to come. Once they heard the sounds of the CC130 overhead, they then lit their first flares and each member walked about 30 meters to their right and lit the next flare. This created a nicely visible airstrip for the plane coming in. It was a clear night over Devon Island, with the flares on the ground; a plane could see it long before the plane could be heard. If the plane chose to land the flares needed to be burning not only for the landing, but for the take off as well. But if the plane just dropped the cargo out of the back of the CC130, it was not as important that the flares burned as long. So, without knowing the intention of the pilot, they waited for the sound of the plane before lighting them.

Less than five minutes later, the CC130 swooped down and in the space of less than 600 meters, three large skids landed on the ground after being pushed out the back of the plane mere feet above the ground. This time they were not landing, just what is called a 'touch and go', but the wheels never did touch the ground. Perhaps the pilots didn't know the makeshift airstrip was now clear of objects.

The first thing noticed on the closest skid was a full tractor along with a towable trailer and a towable generator as well. On the next two skids were much needed supplies including several barrels of diesel fuel for the generator and tractor. Along with them were several large wooden crates with rations, cables, strings of lights, batteries, and so much fresh food.

Captain Logan ordered the generator to be started right away even though they had nothing to power up just yet. He knew that if the fuel became too cold, it would not start. It had a small heater to keep the fuel at a useable temperature. The tractor had this feature too, but it also had a block heater, so they could shut it down when it was not in use.

The first crate was opened, and its contents loaded on the trailer. It consisted of general supplies such as batteries, cans of naphtha fuel, canned goods, tools, and several rolls of electrical extension cords and even luxuries like toilet paper, newspapers from Calgary, and most importantly; beer (Captain Logan hadn't ordered the beer yet, so this was a big surprise to him).

The next crate was opened and the smiles lite up the faces of all who could see. There were foldable cots for the entire group to sleep on. There were even heavy wool fire blankets. The blankets got this name because if you were in a fire you could wrap it around yourself and exit the area where the fire was. There were real pillows too. They also received a portable chemical toilet. Also, in the supplies were four portable shower bags that hung up over a metal rig. Now they had all the creature comforts of home.

In the other crates where more fresh rations along with canned rations to supplement the food, a stand-up gas stove, and ten foldable tables with folding chairs. They could now use Melmac plate's cups and bowls, and they could put away their mess tins. Cook was excited to see a wash basin to do his cleaning in (although he often convinced others to do the clean-up). In addition to folding tables for cooking, and serving, there were tables for eating one to use as a desk for the Captain, several chairs, immersion heaters, and may other things to make life there more enjoyable. Of course, the big item to make things comfortable was a four section modular tent that allowed them to have a nice heated common room. This tent had the cooking station, immersion heater, tables and chairs set up, and before long, all the cots were set up as the staff abandoned their arctic tents for the more comfortable heated modular (mod) tent. The diesel fuel drums could be stored inside the tent, so it didn't freeze, even though it is not usually done. Other fuels would need to be stored away from the tent.

While all these goods were being unpacked and loaded on to the trailer for a few runs back to the bivouac site, Captain Logan came to the realization that they were going to be there a very long time. Although he knew this before, now it really dawned on him. This concerned him too. He had discussed this possibility with his staff, and they were well aware, but he never did comprehend the overall length of time needed to complete this mission, now it was becoming real to him. He wondered how long this assignment would actually be. Likely much more than six months as it would not even be light out until that time.

After about two more hours had elapsed, all the items were back at camp. It took just over one hour to set up the mod tent and soon after the immersion heater was installed and running. Some soldiers wasted no time in getting their cots set up and a pillow in place at the head of their makeshift beds. Others helped Cook stow away all the food and set up the new stove and wash basin. A corporal voluntarily stepped up to act as the supply staff, logging what came in and what will go out and used up, so when necessary, new supplies will be ordered. The Warrant officer drew up the fire picket list and decided with Captain Logan that they would both take a shift in the middle of the night, one after the other to allow the group to have an extra-long sleep. Two more hours were added before reveille. After all, they were all up much later than normal, and in the arctic, you burn far more calories due to the cold.

On this night there would be eight people doing a one-hour fire-picket shifts. When Captain Logan was doing his shift, he saw just how tired his group really was. He was so proud of his men. He had remembered something he learned as an officer cadet just a few years earlier. 'If your subordinates know you care and they know that they are your priority over anything else, they will make you look great. But if you want to look great by trying to care for them, they will see through your feeble attempt and you will fail." He also knew to never ask them to do something he wasn't willing to do himself.

Chapter Eight

Take the craft

November 1st, 1966. It has been almost one month since the crew at PIN-4 first notified Winnipeg and NORAD of the blip on their screen. Any attempt to get more information had been denied. Ron Kay was ordered that it was a non-issue and to let it go. Of course, with him being the inquisitive type of person that is like begging him to investigate further.

Ron knew some people in other positions and felt he could get more answers once he is rotated out of PIN-4. But that was still months away. Also, he needed to be certain of who he asked and what he asked. He didn't want this to come back to him.

Back on Devon Island, Captain Logan was concerned about the instructions he received from NDHQ (National Defence Headquarters). At first, he thought he was there to help the aliens make the necessary repairs, if that was even possible. But now he learned that his goal is to dismantle the craft, so it can be taken away for study. All the materials, tools, foods and even medical supplies would be examined and studied carefully. This may even include the alien's themselves. This was a thought that frightened Captain Logan.

As one could imagine, this caused quite a bit of stress for the captain. He cared about these aliens, and the fear of them had all but subsided with him and also with his team. He had also felt a loyalty to his country. The technology these aliens possessed could help Canada be a world leader in so many areas. Of course, he wanted to be part of that, but he feared that it would be viewed negatively by the aliens that he now came to care about.

Captain Logan decided to walk to the craft. His staff was there studying what they could of this machine. They were taking pictures and documenting everything that they were able to see. As he approached the craft, he ran into their commanding officer Scara, he wanted to tell him of his new orders, but didn't know how.

Scara commented through thoughts; "I see you are troubled. As I told you before, the damage is unfixable. My crew and I will assist you in dismantling the craft for transport, but I would like to know what is going to happen to my people?"

"I will make all inquiries and get back to you, Scara. Unfortunately, I really have no idea" Instantly he felt relief knowing that he did not have to deceive the aliens, and he could not be accused of handing over protected information to them either. But he still felt bad for the things he did not know. Now he had to think of what was needed to dismantle the craft. What new tools would be needed, and how long would it take.

"The easiest way to dismantle this craft is to cut it down. But you cannot use high heat very easily. Our craft is well built for the extreme temperatures we may face. The only way you can cut this craft is to use a fine stream of high-pressure water." Replied Scara, already knowing what Captain Logan was contemplating. "Inside it can be cut with your cutting torches, but the outside skin of the craft is a metal that requires much more heat. Also, it would melt more than cut if you could actually get a torch that hot.

"It will be a long time until we can do that. We are months away from daylight. And the temperatures will not get above freezing until after then. I am guessing we are all going to be here for a quite some time."

The Captain made a mental note of another item to put an order in for. He had never heard of a high-pressure metal cutter using water, but this was not his area of specialty. Combat arms were his expertise. As he thought about it further, he would need a water barrel, but not just any water barrel, one that had the capacity of a small pool. And then there would be hoses and water pumps. The hoses posed a concern. As everything was frozen, where is the nearest source of clean running water going to come from? How much hose will be needed? IN addition to the water cutter and all that goes with it, he would need cutting torches, with several tanks of gas, plus written information on how to use this equipment.

Captain Logan now knew that over the next few months, they would just be getting ready for their real assignment which could not start until the late spring. Between now and then, they would just have to do the preparations required for the task. These preparations would include one by one removing everything from the craft and logging the item and photographing the item. Once everything is removed, they could use the cutting torches he would order to cut the internal structures. Then once the sun comes up and the temperature was above freezing, they could commence the final cutting of the craft to have it taken away.

In the last drop of supplies, there was a pop-up mast used for stringing the antenna wire with. This improved their signal by a huge margin, but it also allowed for a make shift flagpole. Previously the Captain had his NCO's (non-commissioned officers) task a couple soldiers with setting up this pole so they could raise the flag. Even though it was always night time. It was the new flag of Canada that was less than two years old. With Remembrance Day coming up, Captain Logan decided they would have a small service. The aliens were invited, but they rarely left their craft for more than half an hour.

Scara explained that it is getting too cold for them to spend any significant time outside as they are from warmer places than this.

"Well Scara, it is too cold here for me and my staff. Thank god for the heaters we have in our quarters now." Captain Logan made a mental note about requesting roughly forty smaller sized arctic jackets.

"That would be nice. The jackets would allow us to spend more time outside the craft."

November 11, 1966. At 10:30 AM local time, Captain Logan had assembled the staff to March to the flag for a small Remembrance Day service. Once there, formed in three ranks, they were about to start a small service. They did not have a trumpet, there would be no fly-past, no reviewing officer, and it would be pretty short. They all knew this was a proper service despite the lack of spectators too.

As they formed up in front of the flag pole, they could hear the sound of shuffling feet moving towards them. It was the entire group of aliens with the exception of those injured or those caring for them. They were wearing their new Canadian Forces Parkas that arrived just two days before. But these parkas fit them like potato sacks, and it was hard for the soldiers to supress a laugh at seeing them almost tripping in their new army parkas. This was especially so when they saw that they didn't fit their bodies properly at all.

The Aliens formed a line behind the Canadian Soldiers. It was clear that they understood the significance of the ceremony, and why it was done. They were very respectful as the flag was lowered to half-mast at about 11:10. At 11:11 everyone observed one minute of silence.

When the service ended, they all went to the modular tents for beers. This was the first time that the Aliens had ever entered the bivouac site. They all sat on either the cots or the chairs by the tables.

Beer was being handed out to the soldiers and offered to the aliens. Finally, one alien decided to try a beer. To him it was far too cold to drink, but after a few minutes in the warm modular tent, it had warmed up enough to be tasted.

Everyone stopped what they were doing to watch him have his first taste of the beer. He put the stubby bottle to his mouth and attempted to take a drink, but these bottles were not designed for alien mouths, and some of it ran down the front of his parka that aliens were all still wearing. Everyone had a small laugh at this. But there was enough beer that did enter his mouth for him to get a good taste.

The soldiers laughed when they saw the expression of disgust on his face. But he continued to drink it. The soldiers received a telepathic message of; "this is good." But they felt he was just being polite. Still, he did finish it, as did the few other aliens who also tried the beer.

It became obvious to the Soldiers that less than a bottle, and the aliens seemed to be getting pretty intoxicated already. The PPCLI medic known as "Doc" became a little worried and approached Captain Logan.

"Sir, we don't know if alcohol is a toxic poison to them, I would suggest we cut them off until we know more."

Before the Captain could reply, Scara came forward and stated that there is a beverage much like this that they drink, and it has the same effect with the same amounts consumed. But he agreed they should stop as there were questions of the safety that needed to be considered.

So, it was decided that for their safety, the aliens who are having beers would be cut off after just one beer. There was some further laughter from this decision, but everyone there agreed that their safety was more important. Still the soldiers enjoyed watching the intoxicated aliens who were clearly enjoying themselves too.

On that day, apart from the usual routine chores, the Captain decided that they could have the day off. Most had beer in bivouac. The potato chips were a huge hit with the aliens. Apparently, it reminded them of a snack from their home. Both Scara and Captain Logan noticed that they were getting along as one group, not two or even three. This was a fact that both him and Scara were very happy to see.

One member of the Rangers was showing off pictures of his wife and home village to an Alien. He even produced a picture of an igloo he had built when his wife and he were doing some traveling over the frozen land. The alien had a hard time believing that you could be very warm sheltered in ice. He was even more impressed when he learned that it can get so warm in an igloo that you strip most of your clothing off just to be comfortable.

Cook was having a conversation with the female alien Pench. They were both showing genuine interest in each other's stories. They were talking about their homes, their childhoods, and what their dreams were. Both were smiling and enjoying their time together. It was rumoured that Cook was having romantic thoughts about this female alien and that she had read it and concurred with it. The rumor further continued that she had put the thought in his head first and because she had the romantic thoughts first. But this may be just an embellishment of the story that night. In any case, there is no evidence that anything inappropriate had occurred between them.

It was also learned through an astronomy map that the aliens all came from Zeta Reticula, which is a star system in our galaxy. This information did go into the weekly report of Captain Logan. However, he did leave out the part about the brief romance between one of his staff and the alien. Some things just don't need to go into a report.

Captain Logan and Scara sat on a cot together. They were talking more about the craft. Once again Scara had stated that the craft is simply not repairable with the technology here on earth. So reluctantly Scara had told his staff that they will not be returning home. But this is something that his crew had already realized without Scara telling them. And fortunately, they all knew the risks when they came on board the craft. Still Captain Logan couldn't help but feel he has some way let them down. Scara sensed this and knew Captain Logan was a good man. He knew that Captain Logan cared about them and the Craft, and that was a comforting feeling to all of them.

So, having them all know this, it was decided that they would assist in dismantling the craft. This would prove to be a huge undertaking. It would require far more equipment, many trips with large helicopters to remove pieces, plus untold supplies. Captain Logan and the Warrant Officer had a huge task ahead of them just assembling the list of needed supplies and tools.

November 12, 1966. All the soldiers got up at six in the morning to conduct their ablutions and have a good-sized breakfast once again prepared by Cook. Captain Logan noticed that Cook was looking a little tired this morning. He feared that Cook needed bedrest and that it was more than simply lack of sleep. He looked a little green. Perhaps he was a little under the weather. These cold temperatures could lower one's immunity.

The medic affectionately called 'Doc' was asked to have a cursory look at Cook. He could not tell much, but as there was no sign of labored breathing, and it resembled fatigue, there was nothing that he could do aside from suggesting the bed rest that the Captain already had done.

Captain Logan asked one private to stay behind to assist him clean up and wash all the pots, pans and dishes so Cook didn't need to. He then told Cook to get to bed and get some rest. Reluctantly, Cook did just that. Although Cook felt that he was not being helpful today, and that was not like him. But he knew he needed the rest.

Once the private and Captain Logan were finished with all their chores and tasks, they proceeded to walk over to the craft site to assist in the work that was being done there.

Items from inside the craft were now being moved outside. Slowly all the smaller items would come out and get sorted and logged outside. There was no concern about moisture as the temperature was too cold and the air was extremely dry. Captain Logan decided that he would direct that the large containers that arrived with other equipment would be used to start filling with these items. So far, they had about eight of them from air previous drops. These were used and filled one at a time. It would take about two months to empty the craft of all its items, plus catalog them and list what was going into each crate. For each and every item, it needed to be logged and described and, in some cases, photographed too. The paperwork was almost as much work as moving the largest pieces out. Fortunately, he learned that there is also a large hatch with a ramp specifically for loading and unloading of larger items. Just like the personnel hatch, when closed you could not see any lines of where it would open.

That evening the crew proceeded back to bivouac. They were all looking forward to another fine meal prepared by cook. They had expected to see Cook working on the food line ready to serve a hot meal. Much to their horror, when they checked up on him, he was dead in his sleeping bag. He was cold to touch, and he was blue.

Captain Logan ordered him removed in is sleeping bag to be stored in one of the empty crates outside. His first concern was that there was something contagious, perhaps even something caught from one of the aliens. A complete scrub down of the bivouac was ordered. This was followed by intense cleaning of each person's clothing and finally for each person individually. Although the cause of death of Cook was not known, Captain Logan knew that they had to treat it as a biological or viral threat that may have been inadvertently brought on by the aliens.

After this long clean-up, a late dinner now consisted of rations being heated up. No one was in much of a mood to volunteer to cook, and even the dinner conversation was close to non-existent. There was a deep sadness that everyone felt. Captain Logan would advise the aliens the following day.

Later, long after the dinner was completed, Captain Logan asked the warrant officer to put together a small service for Cook to be conducted in a couple more days. Then he went to the Teletype set to pass along the news and to order more supplies and equipment. Now this order would include some body bags. He wondered how this news would affect the operation once the staff in Ottawa heard about it. He also wondered about his staff. Naturally morale would take a hit, but he could get past that: Unless the cause of death turned out to be a concern. Time will tell.

Less than half an hour later, he got his reply. Continue with the mission. There would be a military helicopter coming in from a Arctic Research station landing to pick up Cook. This landing will be at 9:00 AM in two days, weather permitting.

For the next two days, it was work as usual for the soldiers. Each day a crew member would volunteer to be the cook for the day. Morale had taken a big hit, but it was starting to restore, still there was a void in the group. Cook was far more liked and appreciated than they ever realized before. Even the aliens were sad too. Especially the female alien, Pench that Cook was chatting with on Remembrance Day. This confirmed to everyone that she had feelings for him that surpassed the feelings they all had for each other.

November 15, 1966. At eight that morning, there was a short service conducted by the warrant officer. A couple others told funny stories about Cook; things that would have embarrassed him if he was alive. But it was all in fun and they all believed Cook would have appreciated it. Meanwhile, about 250 meters from the location of the modular tent where they gathered for the service, there was a large string of lights making a circle that was lying on the ground. The generator, which was several hundred feet away, was all but silent in the distant. Then they heard another noise, just slightly louder than the generator, but it was getting more and more noticeable. It was their incoming helicopter arriving to retrieve their friend.

A short while later, the lights of the helicopter could be seen. The makeshift helipad was doing its Job properly and the Helicopter first hovered about 40 meters away, they could see that there was a large barrel shaped tub suspended from the helicopter. They detached it from the cable and the helicopter moved and landed at the makeshift pad. It was a Boeing CH-47 more commonly known as a Chinook. It was loud, and it was big. But it could also haul quite a bit of weight.

The pilot did get out stretching his legs as well as making a pit stop at their chemical toilet. Once out of the latrine, he approached the Captain and produced a package for him. It was obviously documents of instructions. He was also advised that there were some items on board for them. It turned out to be more equipment. There were three high pressure water pumps, about two kilometers of two-inch hoses rolled up nicely, and there it was, the water cutter he had requested. Now they just needed to wait for the sun to come up in a few more months so the ice here would melt. They also hope they would have enough water to do the Job.

After they had unloaded their equipment, and Cook's body was placed in the helicopter, it took off and left them. The sadness and emptiness resumed, but they also knew there was a Job to do, so like the soldiers they are, they resumed the work at hand with a renewed enthusiasm.

December 3, 1966. The first of the custom-made modular tent pieces arrived that morning. With it was so much canvas and each bundle had a unique number on it. Along with the canvas were stacks and stacks of poles. Included in this was an instruction package that was so big that it looked like a New York City telephone book. The Warrant officer looked through this book. Much of it was hand drawn diagrams. But it was all understandable. Whoever made this book, gave great instruction on how it is assembled. It was also learned that there would need to be at least three more drops before there was enough to complete this tent. The assembly in principal was not very difficult and much like the modular tents they had in their Bivouacs site. The real difference was the size and number of people needed to assemble it.

The group wasted no time in starting the assembly. It was a little different than a standard modular tent, because due to the size and weight, the canvas could never be lifted in place over the frame.

Even the frame required special attention. They had to build it, and with about five people on each leg, lift it and walk it into place. Fortunately, there were special slots welded to each leg that they could attach a temporary lifting handle. The first section they received was the bend in the middle. They assembled the first section. Once it was completed, they lifted it up and walked it down the entire length of the craft. There were ten people on the front of the craft, and ten more at the rear of the craft. Just over half way down the first side, they put it down for a five-minute break. This frame was heavy, but just a few minutes later and the frame was in its place. The next section to make up the elbow of the craft had to be moved into place from the other end of the craft. This time they hauled all the poles by the tractor to the other end. It too was assembled and eventually that frame was in place. A ladder was used to attach the poles from both sets of frames, now making it one frame.

This took most of the day, and they were tired. Tomorrow they would put the canvas over the frame.

When that chore was started, it took everyone to lay out the first tarp on the ground and to line it up for hoisting over the frame. The tent parts that arrived had included a rope with a weight on one end specifically designed for attaching to the heavy canvas so that made this tarp could be pulled over the frame. The other end had the weight attached that allowed it to be thrown over the frame with ease. This weight was called a monkey's fist by one of the soldiers who was into boating as a youth. So before long, they all called it by this name. There were four of these ropes with monkey fists in total for the assembly.

One by one these ropes were attached to the canvas tarp and thrown over the frame. When all four were done, some of the staff walked to the other side and pulled on the ropes until the tarp came all the way over. Then they were secured to the frame, and the first tarp was now in place. An hour later and they knew what they were doing.

All three tarps were now in place and the first section was complete. So, they began working on the next section.

The walk down the length of the craft while carrying the frame was difficult due to the weight of the frame, but they also knew that each time they did it; the walk would be a little shorter. They now had all the sections they received set up and in place. They had to wait for the next drop before they could continue.

December 25, 1966, Christmas day. This was a day off for the staff of Devon Island. They managed to fill several containers of items removed from the Alien craft. In addition, they completed the large tent. The seams of the tent were every fifteen feet, and there was about a foot overlap, so it would not keep water off them when raining, but it would certainly help. But Devon Island was an arctic dessert in some parts, so rain was not likely to occur often. The primary use was to prevent Soviet spy planes and soviet long-range bombers from seeing it once the sun came up. And this task was being accomplished far ahead of schedule. They still had about three more months until the sun came up, and then the ice would begin to melt, and they were nearly ready for this way ahead of schedule. The next few months would allow them to finish removing everything from the craft, pack it up and await the shipping out. Meanwhile more shipping boxes arrived. A request was also put in for parts to build a Quonset hut for the aliens to relocate inside once their craft was no longer usable to house them.

The parts for the Quonset hut arrived and the aliens looked on in amusement as they watched the Canadian soldiers attempt to assemble it. Fortunately, some of the rangers had Quonset huts back in their home villages, so they had a better idea then the regulars did. The Quonset hut would be much better insulated and therefor considerably warmer to make the Aliens feel more comfortable in their new quarters.

Within four days, the Quonset hut was completed, along with a floor and windows. It even had electricity and electric heating and lights. It was not perfectly level though, but it was otherwise properly constructed. More cots had arrived, along with some arctic sleeping bags for the aliens. As soon as the aliens needed to, they could move in.

Captain Logan was surprised to notice that the Aliens seemed pretty happy. This struck him as odd when they knew they would never see home again. They knew that over the years, one by one they would pass away until just one is left, and he or she would have no one of his own kind to be with. This was a sad and morbid thought to Captain Logan, but he knew it was reality.

Scara walked up to him and said; "Thank you for your concern, you have been a good friend to me and my people since the day we first have met, and I will always appreciate you for that. I assure you, we are not the first to come visit your planet, and we will not be the last ones here either. Our craft may be beyond our ability to repair, and we may be stuck here for the remainder of our lives, but we may not be either;

others from my planet may come and find us, only time will tell. There are others here on your planet now. Some of them may have crashed here as well. Eventually we may meet up with them, or maybe not. We may even meet up with others not yet here. But we will make the best of our time here and be happy along the way. Each one of my people came here to make a difference, and by the friendships' we have made, we feel we are doing just that. We all knew of the risks when we left our homes. So, we look at this as just another way we are fulfilling our objectives and goals here. We certainly all feel this way."

February 11, 1967. The remainder of the tent pieces have all arrived with a few more trips of the Chinooks and the CC130's. And with the help of the aliens, the Craft is now completely covered as of this date. In addition to that, about fifty percent of the contents of the craft has been removed, catalogued, and inventoried and was loaded in the containers. Many containers have already been shipped out, but some were still awaiting pick up. Of course, there were several empty ones on standby as things were removed. When the weather is good, the Chinook helicopters will come and take the crates away after dropping off new ones.

February 24, 1967. Today the morale took a small jump at the arrival of a new Hammarlund short wave receiver. Now the group could listen to music and news from around the world. The Aliens seemed to enjoy listening to Elvis Presley as well as other rock music. They also liked to listen to the news on short wave as they could learn about the Vietnam War. This seemed to make them very interested. Captain Logan asked Scara why it was so interesting to them.

"Centuries ago on Earth time, we had many wars were nations fought nations, people fought people. To a small extend we still do."

"What happened to change that? Wars have been fought here as long as humans have existed." Asked Captain Logan.

"If two nations went to war, and deaths were occurring, no nation on our planet would ever do any business with them until it was resolved. Countries quickly learned that war would equate to them starving and running out of many things necessary to their people. So, in turn the people would not fight. If they had disagreements, they could take it to the planets court for adjudication and usually a mid-way ruling would fix the problems. But we haven't even had a court hearing for two nations in many lifetimes."

"I am not sure this could ever work on Earth."

"Not yet, but maybe someday."

In the early evening the group from PPCLI and the Canadian Rangers turned on the Hammarlund and started dancing to the tune of 'I'm a Believer' by The Monkeys'. As they were dancing and having fun, the aliens were watching and laughing. Before long, the aliens were dancing too, although it was described as they looked like they were having seizures with smiles on their faces.

Many friendships have been forged in recent months. Sadly, three of the aliens had died from the initial injuries of the accident. Their bodies were sealed and removed. The aliens thought it was strange to see humans conduct a service for them, but they appreciated the care that the army took. In a conversation with Scara, Captain Logan learned that the Aliens do not have services for their dead. They miss them when they are gone, but it is not viewed as a tragedy, but a continuance.

Captain Logan tried to avoid thinking about the autopsies they were likely undergoing south of here in some secret location. He didn't want it to bother Scara or the other aliens, but likely they suspected this was happening to their friends and colleagues.

The next day, Captain Logan sent a couple Rangers out to scout the area for where there will likely be a stream near the craft once the temperature start to rise to the point where ice would melt. They came back with a report that the only appropriate place they could see would be about seven hundred meters the other side of the craft. More lengths of hose were ordered. Also, the sun was now peaking over the horizon for a little over one hour each day. The temperatures were still very cold, but they were climbing a little.

March 23, 1967. The sun is now over the horizon for most of the day, but it never really reaches very high in the sky. The temperature of Devon Island is rising, but it is still below zero, so the water is still frozen and cannot be pumped yet.

As a precaution, an antifreeze solution has been delivered and added to the large water barrel so that they can start the pumps the moment there is water in the dry stream bed. The antifreeze will also be added at the hose intake to prevent freezing in the lines. The hoses were all in place, everything has been removed from the craft. In addition, most containers have been picked up and removed by the Chinook helicopters. All that was needed now was the temperature to rise and get some water in the large tub for the cutting of the craft to start. The soldiers have read the manuals on how to do the Job, and they feel confident that they can use the equipment. Now they just need water.

Hooks were welded on to the craft at fairly close intervals so that later, when cut to pieces, they could use the helicopters to haul away each piece, one at a time. Of course, they would be wrapped in tarps so that no one, including the helicopter pilots, would know what is being lifted out.

Chinook pilots were a unique breed. As it was the heaviest lift helicopter in the Canadian Airforce, they were called in for all sorts of unique Jobs and they rarely cared what they were hauling. They only cared about the weight, the wind loading and the weather. Taking these to Suffield base did require an overnight stop for rest and refueling. So, the total time was about four days. But the pilots seemed to enjoy these types of challenges.

Chapter Nine

CFB Suffield, Canada's Area 51

Canadian Experimental Station (CES) Suffield, is a station located in Alberta Canada. In 1950 it was renamed the Suffield Experimental Station. Then in 1967 it was renamed again to the Defence Research Establishment Suffield (DRES) and it is the largest chemical and biological weapons research center in North American, and one of only three NATO CBW (Chemical Biological Warfare) research projects worldwide. Because of its normal functions, it was a logical choice for anything that required extra security, and secrecy, already in operation. This became the repository of the extra-terrestrial bodies for study due to the pathogenic containment systems already in place. (This location has often been called Canada's answer to Area 51, although it has never been associated with as many secrets. – Also, this was many years later that it gained this reputation). In 1971, the name was changes yet again and today it was known as Canadian Forces Base Suffield. Prior to 1971 it consisted of just a few buildings and an airstrip a short drive away. To keep things simple, it will be referred to as Canadian Forces Base Suffield or CFB Suffield throughout this book regardless of the year.

When the first of the alien cadavers had arrived from Devon Island back in late October of 1966, they were treated as the highest biological threat level for the safety of all involved. Fortunately, not one of the cultures turned up positive, and no virus were ever detected, beyond those that are normal to all humans. And those were also commonly present here on Earth. Still, in an abundance of caution, the body was stored as if it were a bio-hazard.

In mid-November the body of Cook arrived. Naturally being human the cause of death results would have meant more than they would with an alien who sustained trauma. Obviously, there was more interest in the alien body, but Cook had his autopsy done immediately when it arrived for the safety of the crew up on Devon Island. There where cultures done, blood was examined, organs weighted and all the other usual autopsy practices. In the end it was determined that the lungs were filled with fluid and he died of pneumonia. The culture from his lungs came back as positive for pseudomonas aeruginosa which is a common bacterium for people who die from cystic fibrosis. Although it is not as common for otherwise healthy people to die from pneumonia from these bacteria, it is still one of the most common infectious bacteria present. Combined with the low temperatures of Devon Island, it was determined that Cook had a compromised immunity and it had nothing to do with contact with the aliens. But to be on the safe side, staff at CFB Suffield treated the corpse the same as the alien corpses for biohazards. Despite having found that all the aliens died from their trauma. In addition, broad spectrum antibiotics were sent to Devon Island with the instructions that at the first sign of even a mild infection, the infected person was to start these pills immediately.

A large hanger like building has been commandeered on the base to use as a storage facility. The crates had steadily been coming in and slowly filling this building. At this time no one was allowed inside the building except those dropping off more sealed crates. Of course, there were guards keeping the building secured around the clock, and they had wondered what was in the boxes too. But like the most well-trained soldiers that they were, no one asked questions, at least not officially.

Like most bases in the 1960's this one also had a large underground bomb and fallout shelter. Over the last two months, there was considerable work being done to build a tunnel from the storage building to the shelter. It was not tunneled like most bomb shelters, instead a large trench was dug, concrete poured, and then it was filled in. Also, during this construction, there were reinforcements done to the hanger like building. This included reinforcing the doors, removal of the windows, and making the building very strong to prevent unauthorized entry. Inside there was a double door system installed that only one door could be opened at a time so that you could never see inside past the second door. This also protected further against unauthorized entry. To those doing the construction, they wondered why a building somewhat resembling a reasonable sized hanger would undergo these types of renovations. In the end, this building now resembled a large warehouse with several offices, which is really what it is.

The work here was nearing its completion; it included heating and air conditioning upgrades to both the bunker and the warehouse room. The warehouse building included a new kitchen and some rooms without any windows, despite sharing a wall with the outside. There were electrical upgrades with the generator being converted from main power to backup power. There was a large fresh air system installed with the air both entering and leaving the building going through a UV sterilizer. A few of the construction workers payed attention to the fact that this is not a normal way to build structures and they surmised that it was or something unusual. Fortunately, they too knew enough to not ask questions; if they wanted to keep their Jobs and have future contracts in the future.

Paul Hellyer was a gunner in the Canadian Military from 1939 to 1946 before he entered the life of a politician. In the 1960's, he became not only a Member of Parliament, but also the defence minister under Prime Minister Lester Pearson. As defence minister, he would have access to all the files and would know about the Devon Island incident. It is interesting to note that he openly talks about Canada housing aliens and their spacecraft, yet he never discussed this specific incident. Why would that be? Perhaps this was because he was sworn to specific case secrecy?

Meanwhile back at PIN-4, on March 26th, 1967, Ron Kaye was busy packing up all his belongings and saying goodbye to the other staff at his Dew-line outpost. He was going to be flying home as soon as the plane arrived, and it was unloaded. He would miss PIN-4, but he was also looking forward to seeing his girlfriend he had left behind. His next posting would be back at Canadian Forces Base Cold Lake in Alberta. This was the same base he left to work the DEW-Lines. He would return to his previous Job of instrumentation technician working on the instruments of different aircraft.

Chapter Ten

The dismantling

April 19, 1967 the temperature is just slightly above zero. This made it unseasonably warm for Devon Island and everyone there was happy about this. They knew that once they could start cutting, the work would need to go around the clock. If they didn't finish in time, they would likely be there for another year, and they all wanted to go back to their homes. When inspecting the stream bed, there was just a trickle of water coming down the hill from the edge, but a small team of soldiers had previously thought about digging a big pit to fill with water to pump out. At first the water was a little brown, but as the pit filled, the water looked cleaner. Before long, the pumps could be started. Once started, they could attempt to fill the large barrel. Then the cutting could start.

After about four hours, the pit had filled enough to start priming the pumps. So, the hand pump was started to fill the hoses and the water started to fill them leading to main pump. The diesel pump was started and water made its way to the catch basin. The pit was nearly empty by the time the water hit the large capture barrel. So, the pump was shut down as the hoses were now left primed. But the short time of darkness did not drop the temperatures too far, so it didn't take long to have the pit filled again, then the pump was restarted, this time they ran it for a considerably longer period of time as the pit was filling as fast as they were pumping it out into the capture bin. So, Captain Logan decided it was time to run the high-pressure water cutter. Once they could start the cutting process, they it would be best to continue until the Job were done, barring two problems, running out of water, or breakdowns. The warrant officer also directed about six soldiers to walk up the stream path to pile the blown snow in such a way that it would melt faster so that the work would have a better chance to continue. In only a couple more weeks, they shouldn't need to worry about that as the sun should be up enough to help melt the snow located far up the ridge. But the walk to where snow was located was still someway off, it was close to the edge of Devon Island and the stream ran a very long distance. The soldiers also dug a small trench to divert the melting water into the stream bed to help catch whatever water they could.

An engineer back in Alberta figured that for the amount of metal to be cut, they would need at least four cutters, so before the weather warmed up, they had three more cutters dropped off, along with spare parts, three extra water drums, and plenty more hoses. This tool ran water at extremely high pressures in the thinnest stream. This stream cut the metal at the rate of just over two inches per minute. Even though this was quite fast, it would still take until the next winter's freeze to cut this craft sufficiently for removal to. Fortunately, the used water ran downhill to another hole dug from the ground, so they were able to recycle the used water and filter it to keep the equipment running around the clock.

The crew had not only removed everything from the craft, they had also welded eyelets to the body, so that a tarp could be wrapped around the piece, and it could be picked up by the Chinook helicopters and flown out. Over the coming months, piece by piece was removed and flown out by the heavy lift Chinooks. As it was now light out around the clock, so the cutting equipment was running non-stop without any lights needed. Teams of staff ran the machinery with others learning to do repairs as they came up. Some constantly checked hoses for leaks and kinks, others checked on the pumps regularly, fueling them as needed as well as ensuring they were running properly. Still others learned about metal cutting with water. They all Joked that when this Job was done, they could all have new careers in the civilian world.

July 1, 1967. This is a big day in Canadian History, formerly called Dominion Day, it is now called Canada Day and on this very day, Canada is officially one hundred years old. But due to the amount of work needed to be done, and the three more months of daylight, it was decided that work would need to continue. But there was a nice meal planned for them, served in two different shifts. Barbecued steaks were served on this day. Even the aliens tried them.

It was an unexpected treat for the soldiers, but they enjoyed immensely. The aliens for the most part really enjoyed the steaks too. They commented that there was a food much like it from their home planet. And it too was cooked in a similar manner. The soldiers could only wonder what the creature looked like.

Work continued around the clock every single day without fail. Captain Logan worked out a rotation whereby all the soldiers would get a shift, followed by a shift in bivouac, followed by a sleep break. With each soldier having one complete day off every seven days for a break. During their time in bivouac, the soldiers took on the duties of cooking, cleaning, laundry, maintenance of the equipment and tools, and all the other chores that come up in a field camp setting.

Over the coming months, the work was nearing its completion. August 24, 1967 and Captain Logan and his crew were exhausted for almost one year of solid work. Their families back home were left in the dark as to what was happening with them. The Canadian Rangers were a little more fortunate that they could take some time off and travel to their families for one week. Although most of them didn't go. The Rangers were all warned not to discuss their work, but they assured their families that the pay was worth their time away from home. This made things a little better with their families. Besides, the Inuit families were used to the men leaving for long periods of time, but usually for a hunt and never for this long. So, once they learned that everyone was fine, there was no more concern from their families. The children missed their dads, but they knew they would be back after the work was done. When they were back, they would stay for some time so the children knew they could spend a fair bit of time with their dads then.

When one Canadian Ranger returned after a short break, he brought with him several small stone carvings of a polar bear to be given to each of the Aliens. It was obvious to everyone that the Aliens really valued this gift as something they will always treasure. They had never seen polar bears, but did hear the stories of them, so had an idea of what they were like. The soldiers with PPCLI admired the beautiful carvings and some admitted that they were jealous of them. The Rangers assured the soldiers that later they would send each of them one as well.

It was Late September and it was time to start dismantling the camp. Chinooks had just taken the last of the alien craft pieces away, and the decision came from National Defence Headquarters to vacate the bivouac site and send a replacement crew to dismantle the remaining items as the camp was soon to be empty of all the Rangers, and PPCLI soldiers, plus the aliens and all of the alien craft and contents. Naturally they were all happy that some others would do the final clean up. They had spent more than enough here.

Their last morning of occupying the camp which coincidently was October 4th, 1967, was exactly one year to the day after the alien craft had crashed. Also, a coincidence, there was another event that took effect on this very day as well. There was another UFO sighting at Shag

Harbour, Nova Scotia. This is about as far away from Devon Island as you can get, but still be in Canada. This UFO incident was the reported that there was an impact of an unknown large object into the waters near Shag Harbour, a tiny fishing village in the Canadian province on this same date the crew were set to depart Devon Island. The reports were investigated by the Royal Canadian Mounted Police and Canadian Coast Guard as well as the military (Royal Canadian Navy and Royal Canadian Air Force) agencies of the Government of Canada and even the U.S. Condon Committee. When Captain Logan later heard of this, he wondered if this was a failed rescue attempt by the same aliens as this group. But when he asked them about it, they all doubted it. They didn't believe any from their home planet knew where they were.

So, the rangers on Devon Island packed up and left by Chinook (their larger equipment such as skidoos, sleds etc. had long ago been sent back to their homes by the military). It was bitter sweet for the Inuit friends. They became quite close to both the Aliens and the PPCLI and they knew that likely this would be the last contact with either of that group. But they boarded the Chinook and left while the aliens stayed in their Quonset hut to remain unseen by the pilots. The regular soldiers were out in full to say good bye.

About four hours later, a CC130 landed at the Devon Island makeshift airstrip. It rolled up towards the camp at the end of the runway, and then turned away towards the runway to line up in place for their take off. It took about half an hour to load up the plane will all the personal belongings of the aliens and the main kit of the PPCLI soldiers. All the remaining supplies will be picked up by other military personnel likely arriving later the same day or the very next day (They never heard).

They replacement crew would see nothing unusual. All that was left for them was tear down of the Quonset hut, and tear down of the camp. Then pack it all up and conclude the final cleanup to ensure it looked like no one was ever there. Then they would fly back home to their base. Of course, this was a little unusual as the normal situation would be for those leaving camp to have it packed up themselves. But this was their job so despite some grumbling, they did it anyway.

All aliens and PPCLI soldiers shuffled slowly on the back platform of the CC130. The soldiers were happy to leave and looking forward to resuming life in bivouac, but they too wondered how things would become with their new friends. The soldiers were all concerned that they would be properly cared for and treated well. The soldiers helped buckle in the aliens into their seats, and the ramps was closed and secured.

Captain Logan walked through the plane and entered the cockpit to tell the crew that they are clear to leave now.

"Say Captain, how come our orders were to stay in the cockpit and not look at what you are loading?' Inquired one of the airplanes crew.

Captain Logan needed to think quickly to come up with a cover storey. "They didn't tell you? Well, keep this to yourself, but we have pieces of a recovered Soviet Satellite back there. Don't worry. There is no radiation. We tested for that right away. But you know the military; they don't want anyone to know. So, keep this hush hush. The Russians might want it back." He was proud of himself for coming up with this cover storey so quickly.

The plane's engines started up one at a time, after a minute of fast idle, they wailedd loudly as the plane proceeded down the runway. At first it was very bumpy as it was just a dirt strip made by hand some months before. As it picked up speed, the ride became faster and faster. Finally, they were off.

The flight lasted a few hours and was certainly uneventful, except for some minor turbulence.

Chapter Eleven

Welcome to your new home

It was late in the evening when the plane finally touched down at the airstrip near CFB Suffield in South East Alberta. The plane pulled up close to the end of the runway and the contents loaded on to a deuce truck. Once established that the area was clear of unauthorised people, the aliens too filed out of the plane and into awaiting deuces. It was a short drive to the Quonset hut, but right by there was the bunker which was to become the home of the aliens for the remainder of their lives. The tarps were down so no one on base could see the aliens, but the aliens really wanted to see the base. The first to file out of the deuces were the soldiers who were briefed on how they would escort the aliens into the bunker that was a short distance away. Then the aliens could get settled in for the night and the soldiers could get some bed rest before returning in the morning to see them again. One last army truck was made available to transport the pilots to their temporary quarters for the night.

Captain Logan and his soldiers were relieved in knowing that they would still get to see their friends at the very least for one more day. So, Captain Logan and the Warrant Officer took a few minutes to familiarize themselves with the bunker. Where was the bedrooms, bedding facilities, common rooms, etc. Then they returned to the back of the plane, and together with the remaining soldiers, they escorted their friends into the trucks and onto the bunker. The pilots who were confined to their cockpit and were convinced it was because the satellite needed to be moved into the building adjacent to the bunker, were now free to leave the aircraft.

After some time underground, the soldiers left to go into their temporary barrack to wash up and have the first real shower in one year. At Devon Island they did have an ablutions area set up for field showers, but that is never the same. The base had made arrangements to have a mess hall open late that night, so they could have a nice fresh meal. The cooks didn't know anything about this group, but they did know that they should make it special. The cooks did not disappoint them at all. Later, they retired to the barracks for their first sleep in a real bed in over one year. Not one had to be up for picket, or watch, and they were all asleep within minutes.

Reveille was at 0600 and then the PPCLI soldiers had their first PT in over one year. Although when they were at Devon Island they were working hard, and their overall strength was just as good as before their deployment, the running part of the PT was far below their own expectations. Still they completed it. After the run, they showered and put on their properly cleaned uniforms. Although they did wash their uniforms when on Devon Island, this was the first time they were properly laundered in a washing machine in over a year. They did receive some replacements to their combat clothing due to tearing and wear during their Arctic stay.

Soon after, they were off to mess for a big breakfast. Most wanted pancakes, fresh eggs, bacon and toast. This was followed by all of them being moved into a large room with a couple Generals in there along with Member of Parliament, Paul Hillyer, the minister of defence. In addition to them, there was a retired American General that they later came to believe was General Curtis Lemay (they could not confirm if it was him). The long debriefing sessions had begun. Sometimes they were interviewed individually in separate rooms, sometimes this happened in groups. Sometimes it even felt like an interrogation. It actually went on for several days. But this also allowed them to spend more time with their alien friends between questioning.

When they were not being interviewed, they could bring supplies and food to the aliens in addition hang out with them in the bunker. It was likely that they were the only ones having contact with them so far. And the Government wanted to keep it this way for now. Also, even just the few minutes here and there with the aliens were a welcomed reprieve from all the interviews. The Aliens enjoyed the visits too as they felt a bit confined and uncertain of what was going on.

Finally, after about two weeks of this, they were asked to consider an option. They could return to their Unit to resume their infantry Jobs they had before their time on Devon Island, they could resign from the military (if they had the required time in), or finally, they could be re-mustered to work for the coming years with the Aliens. Fortunately, the military gave them all a couple days to think about it, but only a couple of days.

Those who chose the new Job would have to move to a new community nearby in Ralston Alberta for likely the remainder of their military careers. But after one year in a remote arctic camp, the stability was very appealing to many, and most did decide to take the Job. And Ralston was no were near as remote as Devon Island. Also, military members are regularly moved, and this would give them long term stability. This was a luxury rarely afforded to military members.

Those who left the military would likely return to their former residence or at least the city they came from. They could put this whole ordeal behind them and start a new life in a new career path of their choosing, if they wished.

The remaining soldiers would be sent to their former base or another one to be determined. They could finish off their military careers at the end of their term, or they could sign up for another term and make a lifelong career of it. They all had some choices to make.

On the morning of October 20th, 1967, Captain Logan was directed to come into an office on the base. Inside the office was the Lieutenant Colonel he directly reported to, there was a Brigadier General who he did not recognise, and the Minister of Defence, the

Honourable Paul Hillyer. There was only a minute or two of small talk, then the discussion turned to Captain Logan`s future plans. He was asked if he planned to stay on with the military and his answer was in the affirmative. He was then asked if he would be interested in leading up a small team on a top-secret Job involving research.

With the Job came a promotion to Major. And it was a desk Job that would be more like a civilian Job as far as his work hours went. Captain Logan had to think about this, he had always considered infantry to be his ticket to a command position. He needed to consider a long-term carrier change even though it was with the same employer. When asking for more information he was told he would be leading up a team of researchers and support staff to study this alien technology and to oversee the care of these aliens.

Captain Logan asked why they were considering him. The reply was that he showed good work skills, a good relationship with the aliens, and that the fewer people who know about them, the better. As he was placed in a position that was top secret, they knew he could be trusted. With this in mind, Captain Logan gladly accepted the position and advised them on the spot.

That very evening Captain Logan called for all his subordinates to addend an impromptu staff meeting to discuss their wishes. It seemed like about three quarters of the staff wished to do the same thing as him, and the other quarter either wanted to return to the infantry or to leave the military at the end of their terms.

The first thing in the morning the very next day, the military staff went to the bunker to discuss with the aliens what they were going to do. There were some sad goodbyes for those staff who chose to move on. But for those who decided on a new career path, there was happiness in what the future held for new opportunities between the aliens and the soldiers. There was renewed excitement in a new career direction and continued friendships.

Those who chose to move on left nearly immediately after briefly saying their collective goodbyes. The other soldiers who chose to remain there had to make the necessary arrangements to have their belongings shipped from storage in CFB Calgary to CFB Suffield. The belongings were long ago packed up by CFB Currie due to the need for space. So, all that needed to be done was place their belongings on a transport vehicle and send it to Suffield. This didn't take very long at all.

Another big change was that Captain Logan received his promotion to Major, effective immediately and back dated four months. This made him happy as he had some real money on hand as he hadn't spent a cent in well over one year.

Of the staff remaining at CFB Suffield, most chose to move in PMQs' or Private Military Quarters. They were simple designed houses on military property but outside the fenced in part of the base. Many soldiers attached the Suffield base lived in the PMQs' so it did not attract any attention at all.

During their year on Devon Island, the soldiers had saved up a considerable amount of money from working at a remote location with nothing to spend their money on. With remote location pay, plus while on deployment, you didn't pay for meals, or other things, this allowed them to return with decent pay cheques awaiting them. With their extra money on hand it allowed them to purchase furniture they would never have had back in their barracks. Most of them also bought cars as well. Some even bought brand new ones right off the lot. The Warrant Officer even traveled to Medicine Hat to buy a brand-new Ford Mustang.

Major Logan had also successfully petitioned the senior officers to get most of his men a promotion, but there were still a couple who required short additional training to get those recommended promotions. Morale was never higher amongst these men. They felt appreciated and cared for. The staff were excited about their new duties and the promising future the men had to look forward to. They all knew they were part of something big and they were all proud to be part of that, even if they were forbidden from ever telling anyone about their work.

The new duties they had were mainly twofold. First was to care of their alien guests and support all their needs. This consisted of everything from feeding to medical needs, clothing, entertainment, and documenting everything along the way. The second part of their Job was to log, document and assist the research staff. The research staff were now being vetted by military intelligence and the military police, plus the RCMP were contracted to do this as well. This had to happen before they could begin their work with the aliens. The research staff would be stunned to learn what their work will entail once they passed their vetting. Of course, this was all at the highest security level ever, and they could never be able to talk about it except amongst themselves. Even their own families could never learn about what they did at Suffield Base.

PART TWO

Chapter Twelve

Project Overshot

It was now Monday, December 4th, 1967 and one of the first tasks given to Major Logan and the crew from the PPCLI was to transform the bunker into a suitable and comfortable living space for the Aliens. It would likely be their home for many years until they died, so anything Major Logan could do to increase their comfort and happiness, he would try to do for them. At the same time as this, he needed to find suitable research staff who would meet the highest level of secrecy due to the nature of this work.

The research personnel the Major would need to bring into Project Overshot would need to consist of at least one anatomical biologist to study the aliens themselves, a few physicists whose expertise was propulsion systems and quantum physics to study the craft and some of the items removed from it. They would need no less than one chemist, plus mechanical engineers, metallurgical engineers, and electrical engineers. And this is just to start with. Later they would likely need to hire on others with different specialties than the ones mentioned. Perhaps in the future as more information was obtained, they would even bring in an astronomer, a botanist, and who knows what else could end up being needed. Time will tell what they would need to complete the many tasks and all the projects.

There would be other staff that would need to be hired too, but they would not be aware of the nature of the work in 'Project Overshot' (as it was now called). Examples would be a seamstress for custom made clothing, cooks, cleaners, a laundry worker, administrative personnel, etc. They too would need to have high level clearance, in case they saw or learned things during their employment. But they would likely not be involved in the day to day secrecy of the project.

The building near the bunker had a tunnel built connecting it to the bunker. This was completed just a short time before the arrival of the aliens. This building will house the administration, the kitchen, and laundry facilities for the project as well as the warehouse for the parts of the craft currently held in the storage area. So, Major Logan got the funding for outfitting this building and the items needed to outfit it started arriving shortly after. There were still some renovations needed to complete the above ground portions. But funding for this also got approved right away.

The construction crew was not aware of anything unusual about this building; other than wondering why there was another laundry facility being put in place on base. There was also the construction of three laboratories. They were also confused by the new kitchen facility being added; especially one so close to the base kitchen which building was nearby. Some wondered why there was a kitchen without an eating area. Other than this, the only unusual things about this building was the copper plating placed behind the walls to help electrically shielding things like the electric typewriters that were going to be used in the building once completed. Also, there were very few windows and only a couple doors. This was during the cold war, and precautions must be made to protect this program from electronic monitoring. So, the construction crew simply viewed these as normal cold war precautions, so it raised no suspicions with them. Also, this building was part of the warehouse building and it included a heavy lift crane that ran on rails suspended from the ceiling. Once completed, all the parts of the space craft along with all the contents would be stored here and at the older building which was attached. If needed, they could even try to reassemble some of the pieces, but it was nowhere near big enough building to reassemble the craft completely.

Other unusual tasks had to be done. The aliens needed clothing and they had not yet been able to find a seamstress for this unique project. Due to their unusual size and measurements, it would be impractical to order them all from one supplier. If ordered from one provider, questions would be asked. So, a story was created that there was a family that had a deformed child and needed unusual clothing for them. Several different types of clothing were ordered for one alien, and when it looked like the story was believed, it was repeated all over North America at different small clothing manufacturers. Within a few weeks, bulk shipments were being received at several shipping points in many Canadian Cities, these crates were then forwarded to CFB Suffield.

Obviously, security was always a very huge concern here. Even the laundry staff needed to have a high level of clearance. They never asked about the unusual clothing they were washing, likewise, the cooking staff never made enquiries about the strange meals they had to prepare based on ingredients that would not really be palatable to most people. They all did their Job knowing that the cold war was on and the phrase 'Loose lips sink ships' was still fresh in everyone's minds from only twenty-five years ago in World War Two.

October 5th, 1970 brought with it some interesting situations for all military bases in Canada. There was a terrorist group called Front de Liberation du Quebec or FLQ that had kidnapped the British trade commissioner in Montreal. Things rapidly escalated into further terrorism when the Minister of Immigration and Minister of Labour Pierre Laporte was also kidnapped, and shortly after he was killed. This led to the Prime Minister of the day, Pierre Eliot Trudeau, implementing the War Measures Act which in effect caused martial law in Canada. This was the first time the act was implemented when Canada was not actually at war. With the war measures act came lock downs on the base. Soldiers from all over Canada were recalled from leave and many were sent to Ottawa and throughout Quebec on active status. As most of the soldiers assigned to Project Overshot still wore the PPCLI insignia (and they were attached to them on the books as part of their cover story), someone in NDHQ in Ottawa got the bright idea to send them all to Montreal. For a few hours there was panic surrounding what they would do. As soon they would be deployed and on their way to Montreal. Major Logan called the head of Project Overshot at NDHQ several times but was told repeatedly that he was indisposed and would not be able to reply to his call for some time. Finally, Major Logan convinced the Generals assistant that this was a matter of national security. Within minutes, the staff of Project Overshot was stopped from boarding the plane to Montreal. This occurred at nearly the last moment before planes were set to depart.

The FLQ terrorist group effectively ended in 1970 when another enemy group of Canada was threatening to form. This group was the Black Panthers who had caused havoc for law enforcement in the United States for many years. There was even an incident on May 6, 1972. where four RCMP officers from the 'special O' section had allegedly gone to a barn where there would be a meeting with the Black Panthers and burn it down to stop this meeting. The first two tries didn't work so well, but on the third attempt, they managed to get the barn to burn to the ground.

After the implementation of the War Measures Act was finally rescinded, things continued to run smoothly for some time, but in the mid nineteen seventies, Major Logan received an alarming call from

National Defence Headquarters (NDHQ). His direct superior, one of only a small number at NDHQ who knew of the situation, told him that there may have been a security breach and that they will need to bring in a couple others on board to help investigate. Of course, these additional people would only be told what they needed to know, and nothing more. The troubling problem was that one would have to be a Senior RCMP officer. This posed a problem as NDHQ had no authority over him. The other would be a senior member of the Military Intelligence unit. At least there was still some control there.

Major Logan learned that in mid-March Maclean's Magazine, a Canadian publication on current Canadian topics, ran an article about Ernest Zundel where it was concerned that the author may know more than he let on. It wasn't anticipated that MacLean's Magazine would be overly helpful in the investigation; they tend to protect their sources. Additionally, would the authorities want to ask questions from the magazine? The questions might cause the magazine writers to conduct their own investigation on what is going on at Suffield. This concerned Major Logan and it needed to be avoided at all costs.

Ernest Zundel was a Canadian resident who was born in Germany in 1939 and died there in 2017 but he lived for many years in Canada before finally being deported. In the late nineteen seventies and throughout the nineteen eighties he became widely known in the media in Canada for his preaching that the holocaust never happened. He was profiled in the media quite a bit due to his radical views. Coincidently his application for Canadian Citizenship was denied in 1966, the same year the UFO was discovered.

He was an outspoken advocate for anti-Semitic beliefs. May people at that time felt he was causing so much hurt towards the Jews who had managed to survive the holocaust. Zundel was accurately portrayed as the monster he was by the media. He was not a liked person, and his views were not widely accepted, which turned out to be the best thing for uniting the country on this topic. What concerned Major Logan was the claims that Zundel had made. Zundel claimed that Hitler and the Nazis had developed a UFO and hid it in the arctic only to have it re-discovered years later. Fortunately, most Canadians had already viewed him as a radical nut case, and therefore didn't give too much credibility to the UFO story he claimed. But still they had to ask; did Zundel know something about this one that was discovered? Was there a leak somewhere that needed to be fixed? As most people felt he was a nut case, they did not give his UFO story much credibility. This helped in keeping people from asking questions about what was going on at CFB Suffield.

But the big question on the minds of the staff working on this project was if Ernest Zundel had somehow learned about this project and if so, what was found? Was this just a coincidence made up by a mad man, or did he have some information they needed to find out more. Was there an inside leak that needed to be located? Or was there another UFO yet to be discovered? These questions caused a big investigation conducted jointly by the military intelligence and RCMP Special O.

On one occasion the RCMP officer with Special O and assigned to this case, whom Major Logan only knew by the name Rick, casually said to Major Logan. "You know, I was never fingered for the barn burning."

"Are you saying you were involved in that?"

"I am not saying that. I am saying that there were four people believed to have been involved in the arson incident."

"Was there more? And were you one of them?" asked Major Logan.

"I am not saying that either." stated the RCMP officer.

At this point, the RCMP officer simply smiled and left the room. Rick seemed like a nice and friendly man, but there was still something unusual about him that Major Logan felt he should not completely trust. It was not like he felt that Rick couldn't be trusted with the project, but more like if he said or did anything wrong, Rick would point fingers at the major at the first opportunity he could get.

Throughout the coming months, all the CFB Suffield personnel associated with Project Overshot were re-interviewed, including the original Rangers and the members of the PPCLI who had chosen to move on. All support staff hired on after the project at CFB Suffield commenced, were also carefully questioned and re-vetted. Were any of them either anti-sematic or anti-government? Did any of them have contact with Zundel? Was there any association with a radical group, or did they have family who were? Or, just as concerning, did Ernest Zundel have information on a real Nazi UFO? The Military could no longer rule it out as there is proof to them that these craft really do exist. Perhaps the RCMP portrayed them as crazy people. Certainly, craziness would be believable in the case of Earnest Zundel. The bulk of Canadians felt he was a nut case and a danger to our citizens especially the Jewish community.

The investigation took a few months, it involved several interviews, sanctioned breaching of offices, wiretaps, and observations in addition to countless observations and investigations of paper trails. By the time the investigation was concluded, the determination was that Zundel had no inside information. Now the RCMP was interested in learning if there was any truth to the Nazis' having this equipment, and was it in the arctic? It may have seemed far-fetched to some, but the RCMP were well aware that there were so many items (mostly art and gold) that left Germany near the end of World War Two, that it was conceivable that some of it ended up in Canada. Also, it was common knowledge that the Nazis had worked on many clandestine projects throughout their reign that there was a possibility that something was in fact there. The Nazi Bell was one such example of clandestine projects they were working on and the RCMP were aware of this project, so they could not conclude that there were no other projects yet to be discovered. The Arctic is so vast that there was no way they could conduct a full and complete search of all the locations a Nazi project could be hidden.

The RCMP did end up learning of the location of a Nazi weather station. The station was located in 1977 when Peter Johnson, a geomorphologist working on an unrelated project (suspected to be on behalf of the RCMP, but not proven), stumbled upon the German weather station by chance. Around the same time, a retired Siemens engineer named Franz Selinger, who was writing a history of the company, went through some papers and learned of the station's existence. He contacted Canadian Department of National Defence historian W.A.B. Douglas, who went to the site with a team in 1981 and found the station still there. It was called Weather Station Kurt and was brought to Ottawa and is now on display at the Canadian War Museum. Originally it was installed by a U-boat crew in October 1943 in what was then 'Labrador, Dominion of Newfoundland'. It is believed that this weather station was placed there by a U-Boat crew to send information on the weather so that they would have a better way to forecast weather in the North Atlantic.

Coincidently, it would likely have been the Siemens Corporation who would have built a 'UFO' style craft for the Nazis'. They build many high-tech devices for the Nazis' before and during World War Two, including the famous 'Enigma Machine' for sending and receiving encrypted messages. As this machine was a marvel of technology at the time of the invention, it would not be far-fetched to believe that other creations from Siemens would also be ahead of their times.

There was another sighting of a UFO that seemed to have some credibility. In October 1978, Constable Jim Blackwood of the RCMP witnessed a sighting of a flying saucer hovering over the harbour near the town of Clarenville near Random Island Newfoundland. He received this report from the local citizens and proceeded to the location given to him. When he arrived at the location, he was surprised to see that the UFO was still present and quite visible. He had a special high-powered viewing scope which happened to be on loan at the time for other surveillance, which made viewing the craft much easier. The craft stayed in the area for approximately an hour and a half.

Constable Blackwood thought it would be interesting to try an experiment. So, he switched on the roof lights of his police cruiser and then observed the craft appeared to mimic the flashing lights with their own. This made headline news at the time and was broadcast on CBC television and NTV broadcasting in Newfoundland. The craft took off like a rocket and went up high in the sky and disappeared out of view. Two years after this incident, the BBC did a documentary on UFO sightings and included the Clarenville sighting in their broadcast. In later years Constable Blackwood retired to his native home in Stellarton, Nova Scotia, where he tried to put the entire incident behind him.

Major Logan managed to get some of the details about this craft to talk to Scara about it. Scara replied that the shape of the craft was unlikely from his planet but would not elaborate on where it may be from. He did say that it could be from a planet that does not like those from his home planet. But no further details were provided, likely because the identification of this craft was not exact enough.

On another note, the year before, 1977, saw the release of a movie called 'Close Encounters of the Third Kind' where the aliens mimicked the lights and sounds produced by the humans. So, was Constable Blackwood making it up, or did director Steven Spielberg have inside privileged information to use in his movie? There was a suggestion that some had made about Constable Blackwood believing that he made this up based on the movie. Perhaps this is why he attempted to retire in obscurity and put this all behind him. But can we rule out the possibility of Steven Spielberg having some inside information?

Chapter Thirteen

Secrecy kept

It was obvious to Major Logan that maintaining the secrecy of Project Overshot was going to be a huge issue for him. One time when attending the base mess, he overheard some officers, who he did not personally know, talking about some weird stuff going on at the old bunker. They had no idea who Major Logan was, as he was still wearing the insignia of the PPCLI. Previously he had requested permission to keep him and his men associated with the PPCLI as their cover story. His superior in NDHQ loved the idea and from then on, he and his staff were to permanently retain the association with the PPCLI and wear their insignia. Although off the books, they were their own unit. Funding was done through the books of the PPCLI to assist in maintaining their cover story.

There were other issues throughout the years that the team at CFB Suffield needed to contend with. 1982 in Canada was a very big year. On July 1st, 1982, the holiday known as Dominion Day was officially changed to Canada Day. Also, in 1982, Canada was to receive the Constitution Act. With this act, Government transparency and how to keep this information quiet, had quickly became a whole new concern. There was another Act that quickly passed; The 1982 Access to Information Act provides Canadian Citizens and other permanent residents and corporations in Canada the right to apply for and obtain copies of records held by government institutions. The institution must reply in 30 days. What did this mean for the secrecy of CFB Suffield? What was Major Logan's responsibility? He immediately contacted the JAG office (Judge Advocate General) to learn what he needed to do to maintain the highest level of security.

The JAG officer wanted to know more, in general terms, so Major Logan asked his superiors at NDHQ for permission to bring him in the loop for the purpose of developing a cover story. The intelligence section conducted an investigation to provide proper clearance on this JAG officer. Much to Major Logan's' surprise this clearance was not granted. Major Logan was not given any reason why, but he knew better than to ask. He was instructed not to talk to this officer any further about Project Overshot. Also to Major Logan's surprise, the intelligence section did make another recommendation of a JAG officer. They recommended Major named Stan Stefanic from the same office.

Major Logan made an appointment to see this specific JAG officer. Of course, Major Stefanic had no idea why this appointment was to occur, but he was assured by his superiors that it was necessary. He was asked to come to Major Logan's office so that the possibility of being overheard, or electronic monitoring would not be easy.

That afternoon, Major Stefanic made his way to the nondescript building wondering what all this would be about. He entered the large concrete building and thought to himself what is inside this building. He had heard rumors, but the most common one he had heard was that there were parts from a fallen Soviet satellite located inside. Therefore, he was not too surprised to see metal detectors, and the requirement to be buzzed through locked doors. Though Major Stefanic was surprised that he had to turn over his writing pad and he was told that note taking at this time would not be allowed. He mentally asked himself why there was such security for a kitchen and laundry facilities which at this point was all he had been allowed to see. Even that caused him to question the purpose of this building. It dawned on him that he was only able to see a small part of this building, that most of it was out of his view. He wondered what was going on there that they needed laundry and cooking on site. He also noticed the food seemed to have a rather unpleasant smell that he could not recognise.

Major Stefanic got to the office of Logan and knocked on the door. After entry he was invited to take a seat on a sofa. Sitting in one of two chairs was Major Logan and in the other was a Major that was identified as an 'intelligence officer' only. He was presently dressed in civilian clothing and looked more like he was ready for a round of golf.

Major Logan did not like the idea of bringing anyone else into their project. He didn't even like using the term given for the operation which was 'Project Overshot'. He didn't name the project, but felt it was a slight against the aliens who had crashed their craft. Still, he knew the necessity of bringing in a lawyer into the project. And the lawyer needed to be well aware of what was going on there.

For the next two hours, Major Stefanic was briefed on Project Overshot. The briefing started right from Day one October 4th, 1966 with their radar showing the craft, and right through to how they came to be where they are today. Sixteen years later, governments have changed over and over, rules have changed, uniforms have changed, and even a few laws have changed. Major Stefanic was brought on to the project to help with the creation of a cover story, along with being the permanent legal counsel for this project. With 'access to information' laws now in effect, there would need to be a lawyer on board to assist with their issues as they arise. He may even be the spokesperson for the project if it ever became necessary. Major Logan hoped it never would.

By the time the briefing neared the ending, Major Stefanic was mentally spent. He tried to wrap his mind around all he had learned in the previous two hours. Was this all for real? Was he part of some strange experiment? When he left the building, he retrieved his pad of paper from the guard at the entrance to the building and began to make made his way back to his office a few buildings away.

He felt almost weak kneed trying to comprehend all the things he had just learned. He decided to take a walk around the compound a couple times just to get some fresh air. During that time, dozens of thoughts went through his mind. Would he see these beings, or the parts of the craft that had been recovered? He learned that Scara and the others were assisting in the research done on the materials, devices, and what remained of the craft.

Major Stefanic entered the JAG building and managed to enter his office without being stopped by curious co-workers. He sat at his desk pondering all the things he just learned. He wondered to himself if he should get up and leave for the remainder of the day as he was certain that his mind would not focus on anything else for what was left of the afternoon.

As he was just about to get out of his seat and grab his change of clothes when his superior officer entered his office and pulled up a chair to his desk.

"Hi Major, how did your meeting go? Give it to me in general terms only please." He understood how secrecy here worked and sensed this one was of the utmost secrecy.

"It went, well… interesting." Replied Major Stefanic, pausing almost between each word. Obviously giving thought to everything he said.

"I know from experience that this must be a big one. I have been here long enough to know when the secret is one of the highest levels we can ever have. I know you can't say anything, but rest assured I have my secrets too". He said in a matter of fact way, but then added humorously; "No, I am not going to tell you mine". They both had a small laugh at this. "Call it a day, go for a long walk tonight, and get some rest. Tomorrow is another day."

"Thank you, sir; I was actually just about to do that". The major replied. "Besides, I couldn't focus on other work now anyway."

Major Stefanic did just that. He changed his clothing and rode his ten-speed bicycle home where his wife was a little concerned about his unusual arrival time. This was out of character for him. Working late wouldn't surprise her at all but leaving early sure did. She asked him about it his early return, but his response was simply "Lawyer, client privilege. I cannot say anything". She believed that answer, but also knew her husband well enough to know that he was bothered by something he had dealt with at work. She was smart and knew to never ask about privileged issues. Even asking could make her a security risk that could impact negatively on him.

Being a very supportive wife, she made him a cup of coffee and brought it to him. He thanked her and joked that a hard drink might be more appropriate today. She laughed it off, but deep-down thought this too is very unusual for him to say. He was not much of a drinker and typically just liked a beer on a hot day. But still she did not take this as an indication of really wanting a drink, more of how this type of comment was not typical of Stan.

"You know that you can leave the military any time you want and pursue a career in corporate and business law in the real world?" She stated.

"You know I love the military." He replied.

"Yes, but when I see you like this, I have to wonder if it is worth it."

Realizing that she interpreted his attitude that he is involved in something bad, he thought he should correct this. "Actually, this really is worth it. This could be a huge thing for my career and I sure don't want to miss out on it."

"If you say so, I just don't want you to burn yourself out over this. I have rarely seen you this stressed about work."

"I have always planned to enter the military after Law School and stay for my whole career. Then we can afford to retire some place nice".

Chapter Fourteen

Welcome aboard

The next morning Major Stefanic and Major Logan met first thing in the mess hall to start working on their plan to keep Project Overshot completely secret. Aware that they were in a common area, and their discussions could be overheard, their conversations were benign for the start. But after their coffees were done, the two moved to Major Logan's private office to talk about the sensitive things.

Major Stefanic now knew what was being held at this nondescript building and what was located underground, what he didn't know yet was what they were doing there. What was the purpose of all this? He needed to know to see if he could work a plausible cover story. Although he did hear the lie that Major Logan told years ago about a retrieved satellite. He liked the story but how would it justify the huge complex and the taking over of the entire bunker? He needed to either come up with a new story or expand on this one.

"What are you doing with all the pieces of this space craft?" He inquired.

"We have a couple metallurgical engineers studying the metals that come from this craft as they have some unusual properties. For example, some of the metals are lighter than plastic and as thin as construction paper, yet are resistant to bending and have amazing shielding abilities from radiation. Imagine a metal very thin and light, yet able to stop radiation like half an inch of lead? Others are memory metals that always return to their shape, that is why the craft looked nearly undamaged when it was discovered after its crash". He continued: "We have electrical engineers and physicists studying the workings of this craft" Major Logan explained. "It moves by altering the gravity around it, even our physicist cannot figure that one out. I learned from him that Physicists have yet to discover what actually causes gravity. I always thought Newton figured that part out, but I guess there is more too it". laughed Major Logan.

"All the other tools on board the craft are being looked at to see what they do, how they are made and what we can use them for. The beings are quite helpful to us, but with our limited understanding of physics, they can only teach us so much." Replied Major Logan. "Also, there are fabrics to be analyzed. Some of them have amazing thermal qualities for hot areas. They are thin, flexible, and durable, yet will not burn and I could take a blowtorch to your chest and you wouldn't feel anything more than slight warmth. Other materials seem slash proof.

There is microelectronics, and a host of other things. Besides, the aliens are not experts on everything we have here, really only on a few things. For example, you can buy a Winnebago and drive it across Canada, but you might not know a thing about engines, transmissions, or electrical. It is the same situation with them. They have a beautiful spacecraft and fly it around the galaxy, but not know anything more than routine maintenance. Like us adding oil or changing a tire. There are many things they know but also many things they do not know."

"That all makes sense, and that now brings me to ask about the aliens, what are we doing with them?" inquired Major Stefanic.

"We have an anatomical pathologist studying their bodies to see if the internal organs work the same as ours. The anatomy experts are basically writing a book on alien anatomy and physiology. They occasionally draw blood and tissue samples to see things at a cellular level and document what we can learn from them. They study their body systems so that we can better learn about them. But they are strictly forbidden from doing anything that could cause them harm."

He continued: "We also hired a vetted astronomer to ascertain where they came from. Although he didn't meet with the aliens, and he didn't know anything secret, we wanted to keep him from talking. We found out that they are from Zeta Reticula which is an area nearly 40 light years away."

"Has anything been done using this technology?" Inquired Major Stefanic.

"As a matter of fact, there has. Canada developed some technologies for use in military, medical and space exploration. Do you recall the Canadarm?

"Yes", replied Major Stefanic.

"Well on November 13 of 1981 the Canadarm was deployed aboard the Space Shuttle. This arm used metals and motors that were reverse engineered from metals on the craft. The motors used to move the arm are small yet extremely powerful. These too were developed from parts found on board their vessel. We could never have developed it as strong as it is with the technology we had today. And as we speak, newer versions of the Canadarm are being developed.

"With them being stuck here all the time, what do the aliens do day to day?"

"Sadly, they are self-imposed prisoners. They can't leave for fear of being attacked by scared people. They know that to come out of hiding would cause world-wide panic. So, they have taken up some interests. Their assistance in understanding the tools and materials is very helpful. They love television, and watch shows frequently. It also seems they like rock and roll music."

"So, these unfortunate aliens must remain underground constantly? Don't they hate that?"

"As humans we would; we would feel like it is a prison. But this underground bunker is bigger internally than their huge spacecraft was. It is just on more levels. Therefore, there is plenty of room in there. And they say that they expected to remain on the craft for the bulk of their life, so there is no complaining from them about the restrictive size of the underground."

"How about the food they eat? What do they like?" Inquired Major Stefanic.

"With the assistance of dieticians, we managed to get a list of ingredients that they explained were similar to ingredients they had at their home planet. This took us considerable time to figure out. We also had some of their foods chemically tested to see what is similar here. From that list of ingredients and consultation with them and dieticians, we came up with a meal we like to call 'Manna from the heavens'. Our dietitians feel it is very nutritious to them, but humans seem to hate it, and I am not sure how nutritious it is to humans. We have found that the aliens developed a liking for human condiments; Particularly Tabasco Sauce. And love to put hot sauce on their manna."

Major Logan decided it might be a good time to introduce Major Stefanic to the aliens. "So, are you ready to meet them?" He asked.

Major Stefanic replied in a nervous voice; "I guess I have to sometime, might as well be now." Although the Major did look considerably nervous and uncomfortable at the thought of the introductions, he knew now was the time. Major Logan understood the apprehension of meeting them. He had felt a similar way years before at Devon Island.

"Just so you are aware, they talk through putting thoughts in your head and they listen to your thoughts. They can even feel your emotions. So, try not to think anything bad, and don't be too scared of them. They will laugh at you;" chuckled Major Logan.

Major Stefanic followed him to the entrance at the back of the warehouse building. Once there, he came to a second security screening area. This time he was given a cursory pat down in addition to the metal detector to ensure that no recording devises or small cameras like the famous Minox micro camera of the time were, on him. Then they had to sign in, and Major Stefanic was handed a second visitor pass to clip on to his uniform. They entered a locked door and walked about ten feet to another locked door that could not open until the first door was secured. Once through the second door, they proceeded to an elevator and went deeper down underground.

The elevator opened up at the first level underground.

"How deep underground are we?"

"It is not as deep as you think, only about thirty-five feet from the ceiling of this room to the outside. But the elevator is an old industrial type, so it seems we travel much farther than it actually does. They were designed for very heavy loads, not for fast speed. Wait until we get to the lowest level. This is only level one. The lowest is level twelve, but there is very little down that far, mostly old machinery from when this was a fallout shelter. The bulk of the aliens live on level nine. And couple of them are on Level ten."

Once they left the elevator, Major Stefanic observed that the walls and hallways were very brightly lit and painted white. There was some generic artwork mounted to the wall every so often. There were even some fake potted plants along the corridor. It was a cheap attempt at making it look less sterile, but it did work. He needed to remind himself that this was the home for several aliens and that real plants may cause problems in either growing them, or worse, negatively impacting the health of the aliens themselves.

"This floor houses mainly the labs. Some of the aliens living here come up to work alongside the scientists hired at this facility."

"What are on the other floors?" Inquired Major Stefanic.

"Well, level two is mainly offices. I have another office on this level too. Level three is a hospital floor for them. You would be impressed with it, it is very well equipped. Of course, we do not have a doctor on staff. If needed, we have a team of veterinarians available for consultation. Fortunately
we have never needed to call them in. So, they likely think we are just treating our lab animals. They will likely wonder what type of animals we have when we refuse to tell them;" Laughed Major Logan. "Level four is their offices, and work rooms. Level four contains a well-stocked library for them. They love learning about world history, Earth

geography, and anything else they can about this planet, their new home. Level five is an exercise room with a short track for running, as well as exercise equipment they designed".

"How big is this place?" inquired Major Stefanic; "A short track, how long is it?"

"It is a loop shaped tunnel that is used for its original purpose, and that is for exercise. The track is a loop approximately 250 meters long. In the center is the elevator and the exercise room. It is kind of shaped like a round tube underground. I sometimes do my running here too."

"What about the other floors here?"

"Level six is their lounge, kitchen, and a boardroom. Level nine is their living quarters for most of them. Their management staff occupies level eight. Levels ten through twelve are essentially unused or used for storage and machinery. There are still air scrubbers and diesel generators located there for fallout conditions, but they are pretty much unused."

"Can we go down to level six?"

"I will phone down there and see if they will meet us in their boardroom. As this bunker is really their home, I like to give them the respect of not just walking in their front door whenever I choose." Major Logan picked up the wall phone and called down. They could now speak and hear in English after spending so much time watching television and listening to the soldiers.

"Scara, this is Logan. Feel up for a visitor? Sure… Yes, I will bring the coffee."

Major Logan told Major Stefanic that he called and spoke in voice, but if they were in the same room, Scara would have listened to his thoughts instead. The two proceeded down to level six and went into the kitchen area to fetch coffees for all three of them. In there, Major Stefanic got his first look at the aliens. There were four of them sitting around watching CBC on their television. The aliens needed to listen as they couldn't do it telepathically with an electronic box. Actually, they have come to really enjoy watching nearly anything on television. This even included daytime soap operas. But one of their favorite shows was 'The Muppet Show', but by now they were all reruns. They had mastered the English language relatively quickly, with some of them going on to other languages as well.

With coffees in hand, the two officers proceeded down the hallway to the boardroom and were greeted by Scara already in there. All three sat down after introductions where made.

Scara could sense that Major Stefanic was thrilled to be brought into this secret. He could also sense that he would have his best interests as well. The explanation of why Major Stefanic was there was given to Scara. So, he knew that this was all about maintaining their cover and ensuring that they would be safe. Scara certainly had a sense of contentment knowing that Major Stefanic was also very devoted to their safety and security.

The three discussed issues about the changes in the laws, and how it could potentially affect them. Also, a cover story will need to be created, but it would not be used unless there were questions coming in from others that needed to be addressed.

Scara liked how Major Stefanic invited him for his thoughts and ideas, rather than just come in and dictate how things would be done. By the time the meeting was concluded two hours later, the two majors felt that new friendships were now forged.

Chapter fifteen

Promotion for the Major

September 3rd, 1985. After nearly eighteen years of running Project Overshot, Major Logan previously applied for a promotion and at a ceremony on the parade square that day, he was called forward and awarded the new rank of Lieutenant Colonel. Lt. Col. Logan took all the staff under his care out for drinks that evening. It is military tradition that he does this, but only for other officers at the officer's mess. Typically they do not do this for his enlisted staff, but although it cost him a few dollars, he believed in taking care of his staff, and they respected him for it. He even gave the speech that it was them who made him look good enough to be promoted. He then thanked each and every one of them for their hard work. Others had been promoted during those eighteen years. The Warrant officer became a Master Warrant officer about three years before his retirement.

It was at this bar seated amongst his long-time colleagues and friends that he was asked what his future plans were. Only about half of the PPCLI staff who came over to Project Overshot was left there. Some new staff has come into the project, and others retired. It was sad for all when someone retired as they knew they would never get to see the aliens again. And they had become more than friends, they were now like family. And the moment you retire, you lose all security clearance to come for a visit.

Lt. Col. Logan said at the bar that he planned to put in about two more years, and then he would retire. He planned to relocate to Vancouver Island, and he wanted to get waterfront property and be able to see the whales swim by. Living more than half his life on military properties had long ago lost its charm. He had married some years back and his wife was yearning for a house to call their own. They had saved quite a bit and figured that their finances were in order to see to their dreams come true in a couple more years.

It was that evening that Lt. Col. Logan thought about who would replace him in this capacity. His first idea was Major Stefanic, he was a JAG officer. Could a JAG officer do this Job? But he also knew that Major Stefanic really did like the aliens and he cared as deeply about their wellbeing as he did. Would he leave JAG and come in full time to head up Project Overshot? It was time for him to discuss his future plans with his superiors at NDHQ. He would schedule the call for the next day.

September 4th, 1985 started out as a typical day. Lt. Col. Logan arrived at work early in the morning, expecting to go to level five and have a morning coffee with Scara. But on his way in to the building he was stopped by the security staff and told that Scara was sick and likely not going to live through the day. Apparently, he was fine through the evening, but in the morning when checked on, he had the same symptoms of other aliens who are near death. They had already had a small number of deaths and were down to just sixteen left.

Logan bolted past the security and ran to the elevator. The other security staff knew what had happened so none of them tried to stop the Lt. Col. for breaking the usual security protocol.

Upon Lieutenant Colonel Logan's arrival at level eight, he went right to Scara's room. Scara was laying in his bed and being attended to by one of the alien medics. The three had a conversation about how Scara was doing.

"I am old, I have had a long and interesting life, but more importantly, I have made the best friends here I could have ever hoped for;" replied Scara. Lt. Col. Logan noticed that even telepathically the messages received from Scara seemed laboured.

"I too have made a good friend in you along with your entire crew. Years ago, when we all first arrived here at Suffield, I needed to make a decision about my career. I chose to make this project my career and I have never regretted a single minute of it. The friendships I have made with you and your crew are the best a man could ever hope for. I feel like I am making a difference for many people here. You will always be my friend."

With that remark, Scara closed his eyes for the last time. Lt. Col Logan felt a part of him ripped right out of his chest. He could hardly breathe and needed to get above ground right away to get some air. He also needed to notify National Defence Headquarters right away.

He returned to his office and closed the door to give him privacy for the phone call. But once the door was closed, he couldn't help but let the tears flow. He realized then and there that he had actually lost his closest and longest friend. There would be a void for the remainder of his life.

By about ten that morning, all the staff who knew of the aliens were now aware of Scaras' passing. There was a deep sadness that befell the worksite and not too much got done that day. But Lt. Col. Logan did get a phone call through to his superior at NDHQ. After giving the initial report, talks switched to a discrete service for Scara, to be held underground of course. Then Lt. Col. Logan had discussed his future retirement that he was now planning for about two years away. This would be when he need to mentor his replacement and bring them in on all the secret information needed to do the Job properly.

Brigadier General Brent (Joe) Kornago was the superior who was handling Project Overshot. They had spoken literally thousands of times on the phone, but they had only met face to face a few dozen times. Although a little older than Lt. Col Logan, he acquired the nick name of 'Joey' as he really liked the punk band 'The Ramones'. Some of his staff even called him Joe, at least when others were not around to hear them. Once for a Joke on Halloween he came to work with a long dark-haired wig and dark glasses dressed looking like Joey Ramone. His staff loved it as it was so out of character for a Brigadier General to do this, and in particular, this General.

General Kornago asked Lt. Col. Logan who he had in mind to replace him as the officer in charge of Project Overshot.

"I thought about that, the very first person who came to mind is Major Stefanic from JAG. That is who I would recommend as my replacement. He is somewhat aware of the things going on here, and he is a good man who will keep the interests of both his country and the aliens in mind. He is smart and will take no time at all to learn what he needs to do the Job. And I have all confidence in him for this job."

"If you tell me that you have all confidence in him, I believe you. Talk to him and see if he wants the Job. If he does, I will make sure it happens."

"Thank you, sir, I really appreciate that. Just one more request, could you arrange for all flags at CFB Suffield to be put at half-staff for the remainder of the day, and all day tomorrow?"

"Consider it done."

Lt. Col. Logan left the warehouse building and proceeded to walk to the JAG building. Upon entry he asked if Major Stefanic was in. When advised that he was, he then walked to the appropriate office and asked Major Stefanic to grab his jacket for a walk.

"This sounds important." Replied Major Stefanic

"It really is".

Let's go." They left the Jag office with little conversation, but they both noticed that the flag in front of this building was getting the flag lowered right then.

"I wonder who died?" Commented Major Stefanic.

"It was Scara, about two hours ago."

"Oh my God, I am so sorry to hear that. I really liked that guy."

"Me too. That was the first thing I was going to tell you. But I also have something else that is important to talk to you about."

"This sounds very important."

"It is. I have something to ask you. I have advised NDHQ that I plan to retire in about two years."

"Good for you, I have several more years to go. My wife is looking forward to me getting into a corporate law firm after I leave the military."

"Well that makes this even more difficult as it will directly affect you and your wife's future plans. I need to find a replacement for my position and bring them on board soon to start the hand over with all the data that has been accumulated. You have already passed the clearance, and you have met the people, so naturally you were the first to come to my mind. Besides, you care about them the same as I do. And that is the most important requirement for me to consider."

"How long do you need before I give you an answer? I need to give this some considerable thought. And I should talk to my wife too. She will have to live here a few more years, and she longs for the big city. Don't worry, I will not tell her about what we do."

"Please, take all the time you need, but no more. If you decide against taking the position, I will have to search for someone else, and then bring them up to date. I should get back to work now as I have so much work to do especially with Scara passing away this morning. Thank you for your time and we will talk again soon." With that the two officers parted and Lt. Col. Logan started walking back towards the warehouse shaped building. Passing by the base commanders building he was stopped by the Base Commander himself. He was an ornery old man named Colonel Al. Mouldy. Sadly, most people didn't respect him much as his arrogance was very noticeable. But deep down, he could be relied upon to do his Job.

"Why did you get NDHQ to order our flags to half-staff?"

"You know I cannot answer that directly, I can only say that one of our people had passed away and he was well respected"

"I don't like it and wish you didn't do that."

"Duly noted sir;" Replied Lt. Col Logan. His voice nearly revealed that he was disgusted with Mouldys' attitude.

"I phoned NDHQ to get permission to raise the flags back up and was told on no uncertain grounds that you would get this request granted and not me. Son, I don't know who you know there, but whoever it is, they have your back in a big way."

"Yes sir."

"That actually tells me quite a bit about your character. Keep up the good work, whatever that work is soldier."

"Thank you, sir." Replied Lt. Col. Logan, now wondering if he had misjudged Brigadier General Mouldy.

Lt. Col. Logan now proceeded back to the warehouse building. A flood of emotions now flowed within him. He needed to make arrangements for what to do with Scara's body. He needed to plan a small service, and this was all on top of his regular duties. And of course, he needed to wait for an answer from Major Stefanic.

The next day, Scaras body was removed and sealed in a metal casket and brought to an awaiting vehicle. The staff of the original PPCLI section, along with five of the original Canadian Rangers from up North flew down to be there. They were in full uniform as an honor guard and pall bearers. They loaded the casket on a hearse and with a military police escort it left. Staff of CFB Suffield wondered who had died that they got a military police escort, and the Canadian Rangers as pall bearers, but the truth was that they were there to protect the body, not escort it. Sadly, those of the original group who were no longer part of Project Overshot, were not allowed to go and visit the remaining aliens despite having Lieutenant Colonel Logan petition NDHQ for just that request.

Lt. Col Logan did not know where the body of Scara was being sent to. Brigadier General Kornago had made the arrangement and had something in mind. Likely the body would be stored in a secure facility as did the other aliens who died here.

Chapter Sixteen

Decisions, decisions...

Major Stefanic had just come home from his day on base and sat in the living room with a cold beer in hand. His wife sat close to him. He was not much of a drinker, and it wasn't very hot outside which was when he usually had a beer. But today he did. She curled up next to him and threw an arm over his shoulder to draw him in close. She could feel his shoulder and neck muscles being extremely tense.

His wife Laurie sensed that there was something on his mind and prompted him to talk about it.

He responded; "I was offered a new position; one that is a leadership role and is a position of good challenges and great responsibility. This position is one of great trust and would give me new and exciting career." But he didn't sound very upbeat about it.

"It sounds great. What is the downside?" As she could sense that there was much more to this than he was letting on at this point.

"I would be staying in the military for a few more years than originally planned. Likely when I leave, I would not be able to get the Job in corporate law as you had hoped. I will be doing considerably less legal work if I take this Job. It may affect my ability to get into the law society of another province once retired. It would also mean we will be living here for many more years."

"I see". She said thoughtfully. After a moment of silence, she asked him; "And what would this Job entail?"

"You know the secret project I am working on now?"

"No, I only know you are on a secret project." She said with a hint of a laugh in her voice. "I have no idea what it entails. I know you cannot tell me what it is, and I respect that, but I must admit I am sure curious and have been since your first day on this assignment."

"Well, I would be taking over the secret project. But it may also change our future dreams and the things you wanted to do."

"You know that since you took on this project, I have seen a new purpose for you. A purpose that I cannot describe, but it's like a feeling you are doing something really big, something really great. And not just for you, something great for the military, maybe even Canada. I sense that this is big, and you want to be part of it. Am I right?"

"Yes, you are right. You are very right. You know me well. Maybe better than I know myself."

"Then I think we should stay here a few more years. I want to see you retired with no regrets. You are a great man and I know you can do great things."

"But I can never tell you about these great things. No matter how much I want to share them with you."

"I understand. You can tell me all about it when you retire."

"No I will not be able to."

Chapter Seventeen

Road trip

The very next morning, Major Stefanic wasted no time in getting to Lieutenant Colonel Logan's office. He was excited about telling him of his discussion with his wife and what decision they came to.. Naturally Lt. Col. Logan was happy to hear of this decision. He was happy because Major Stefanic was both a good choice and also because he wouldn't need to search for another replacement. That could take a very long time and possibly even delay his retirement. Now he could retire as planned.

Later that same day, a call was made to NDHQ advising Brigadier General Kornago about the decision of Major Stefanic to take over the project. No time was wasted releasing Major Stefanic from JAG and reassigning him to Project Overshot. But he would still wear the insignia of JAG as the others still wore the insignia of the PPCLI. This was more to maintain his cover position as was the case with the other staff. He immediately had a new office located in the warehouse looking building. This office was right next door to Lieutenant Colonel Logan's office.

The next week was spent with Major Stefanic at the JAG office with him going over files that were now being redistributed to other JAG members who would be taking over his caseload. Also, other items belonging to the Major were being moved to his new office location. Of course, everything being moved over to the new office would need to be inventoried by the security personnel. But this was pretty routine considering the nature of the office. The others in the JAG office, including his superior felt a level of jealousy despite not knowing anything of his new job in the military.

By October of 1985 Major Stefanic had moved offices and was well underway in his goal of learning all the things that he needed to learn to be prepared for the handover of command in two years' time. Major Stefanic brought with him to the project, not only legal expertise, but some fresh new ideas. One of the first things he did to properly introduce himself to the remaining aliens was to rent a bus with heavily tinted windows and take them on a long drive to Calgary for a bus tour. This was their first time outside of the bunker in years. They enjoyed it so much, that Major Stefanic decided they should do it every summer when the weather was nice.

Getting to see Alberta, even if only though tinted glass windows was a huge treat to the aliens. They had remained underground for so many years that they had all but forgotten what it was like to see sunlight, sky and ground. It was obvious to Lt. Col. Logan that Major Stefanic was a fantastic fit for this Job. He knew that he would be leaving here with the aliens in good hands. There was an almost childlike excitement that was shared by both the aliens and the staff alike. Lt. Col Logan felt this trip was long overdue.

There was so much more for this excursion to take place than most would ever understand or comprehend. The logistics of it and the operation order was so many pages long. He had to get authorization from high up that even allowed for the vehicle to be unsearched when both leaving and returning to the base. This meant that the guards at the base exit and entrance could not search the vehicle as was their routine procedure to do. Two military police vehicles were required to accompany the bus at all times. In the event that the Bus was stopped and subject to a police search along the highway or within the city, the military police would need to prevent the civilian police officer from checking the bus. But fortunately, this never happened.

Lieutenant Colonel Logan was very happy to see how Major Stefanic was integrating with the aliens, and how he was sliding into his new position so well. As second in command, Major Stefanic was doing a spectacular Job of running things. Lt. Col. Logan knew he would be leaving Project Overshot in good hands and that the alien friends were enjoying this new officer.

Chapter Eighteen

Goodbye Lt. Col.

It was a sunny Sunday on November 1st, 1987. A crowd was starting to assemble at the outdoor parade square were soon there would be a small change of command parade for Major Stefanic to officially take over all the duties and operations of Project Overshot. The purpose was also to say good bye to the outgoing Lieutenant Colonel. In attendance was Major Stefanic's' wife, Lt. Col. Logan's' wife, Brigadier General Kornago who flew out from NDHQ in Ottawa, and several others from Project Overshot.

Once the change of command parade was concluded, there was a late lunch reception that carried through to the early evening. Then the next day it was back to work as usual. There was a sadness that Lt. Col. Logan felt as he knew that after this coming Friday, he would never see his friends again and this included both the soldiers and the aliens. He spent twenty-one years of his life with these friends. He cared for them all as if they were his very own family, which in some ways they truly were. Once retired, he would instantly loose his security clearance and privileges, so he could never even come back for a social visit. This made retiring even harder as these people, both the staff and the aliens, meant the world to him. But deep down, he knew that it was his time to move on and start a new chapter in his life.

The next couple days were spent taking care of the paperwork for the handover, as well as his upcoming retirement. This time the work was bitter sweet. One by one, all things to do with Project Overshot was to be signed over to Major Stefanic. With each passing signature, Lieutenant Colonel Logan felt like he was signing away a part of his life. These signatures included signing over the building, all the contents of which needed to be logged and inventoried as well. Then the bunker and many of the items that were in there. Fortunately, only the secret items and any equipment over two thousand dollars in value needed to be signed over. This made it faster than it could have been. Office equipment didn't need to be inventoried.

The personal items owned by the aliens were their own things. Nothing of theirs needed to be signed for. Some had purchased small TV's for their room, others had purchased music systems. Major Stefanic found it very amusing that he didn't have to sign for their items, but he had to sign for the aliens themselves, as if they were military property. But he understood the way the military works and just laughed to himself.

Wednesday, Thursday and Friday, Lt. Col. Logan spent the time saying good bye not only to the aliens, but to all of his subordinates. Some of them had been with him on Project Overshot since before day one, others started much more recently. He made a point of spending a little bit of time with each and every one. There were still several soldiers from the original group, but they had lost almost half of the aliens, likely through old age, but that was never completely determined.

Before he knew it, the last day had arrived. It was a cold and overcast Friday November 6, 1987, Lieutenant Colonel Logan arrived at his office to see Major Stefanic there waiting with two hot coffees in hand. They had some small talk that lasted the duration of the coffees. He told Major Stefanic that he kind of felt numb, like he should feel very different. He had his future retirement to look forward to, but it was hard for him to focus on that. Finally, they got up and Major Stefanic left to go back to is adjoining office.

Lt Col. Logan started to make one last walk through of the bunker saying a quicker goodbye to all the scientists and aliens, he then proceeded then through the warehouse doing the same to both the military and civilian staff. He put his last remaining personal items from his desk into a box and gave the place one last cursory glance. Down the hall he said his final goodbyes to the receptionist Arlene, and to the two front door security staff Rick and Robert. Finally, at 4:00 pm Douglas John Logan walked off the base for his last time. Tears filled his eyes.

Part Three

Selected excerpts of the transcripts of the interviews

Chapter Nineteen

Interview with Ron Kaye

JB   Ron (not his real name), thank you for meeting with me today. I appreciate you taking the time out of your day to see me.

RK   My pleasure. I am retired now so I have time. I spend my day either on my ham radio or restoring older ones. I am not sure how much assistance I can give you on your research, but I am happy to help.

JB   I am certain you can provide quite a bit of information and also you are assisting by filling in some gaps and perhaps by time frames too.

RK   I will do my best. I am an old man now and my mind is not as sharp as it once was. (Said jokingly)

JB   Thank you. I am certain you are just as sharp today as you were back in 1966 when this all started. Could you please tell me about your work with the military?

RK   For sure. I left high school and joined the air force to become a technician. I had an interest in high frequency radio because I have also been an avid ham radio operator, have been for most of my life.

JB   Me too.

RK   Fantastic. I thought in the military I would be working on transmitters and receivers, but I was slotted into other areas instead. After some time, I had completed studying instrumentation to work on various military apparatus. I worked on anything from cockpits of aircraft, to test instruments. It was with this training that I had the opportunity to go north and work on the DEW Line in Canadas Arctic. I thought it would be a nice adventure.

JB   Please tell me what were your duties there?

RK   Mainly I was observing the radar screens and monitoring the radio in search of anything coming from the former Soviet Union or any other communist country for that matter, such as China. Actually, I was also looking for anything that just wasn't right.

JB   Am I correct that you were the one that first noticed the anomaly on the radar, is that what happened?

RK   Yes, but I never officially found out what was out there. I did hear rumors, but I have never been able to confirm those stories. But I can't help but feel there is some truth to these rumors.

JB   I would like to get back to you on what you heard as rumors, but first could you please tell me a bit about what you discovered?

RK   Well, it was a long time ago now. And as I said, I was working in the arctic on the DEW line monitoring both radar and high frequency radio, attempting to intercept long range Soviet bombers as well as any Soviet spy planes, or even missile's coming our way, such as ICMB's. This was during the height of the Cold war. The hours there could be quite long and dull working your shift at the desk. Most shifts had nothing exciting going on. Actually they could be downright boring. We would have a fair amount of commercial air traffic flying over, well for the time anyway. But after a quick check of their flight path we could almost always rule out any hostile plane. Missiles were a threat too, but in 1966 the bigger concern was Soviet long-range bombers. It wasn't even ten years since Sputnik. And that was on October 4th, 1957. So, rockets and missiles were still in their infancy. In the USA they were working on the Mercury and Gemini programs and I think the Saturn Rockets were in their design phase. Coincidently, this was also on October 4th, but in 1966. I saw something on the radar that caused immediate concern due to the fast flying object that presented itself as very large on the radar.

JB   I notice that you seem to recall this date very clearly?

RK   I sure do. You see in addition to this being a very significant radar hit, I also kept a daily log book for myself. I never told my superiors about this log book and to this day they do not know about it, I would likely be in trouble if they knew. The Cold war was a different time for national security. I am happy to provide you with copies of this book, covering these specific dates' dates, if you would like. There may be some subsequent dates of interest to you as well listed in this log book. Just let me know. I can get some copies made for you in a day or two and mail them to you.

JB   Thank you, I would like that very much. Let me know if there is a photocopying cost. I will reimburse you.

RK   Don't worry about that at all. I want to assist you in getting this story published. From what I heard in the rumors, this is quite the story.

JB   Again, thank you. Putting aside the rumors for now, what did you learn?

RK   Well, we needed to ascertain the true size and confirm the hit and that it was not a malfunction of the radar. At first, we thought it might be due to the radar getting a false return. We ruled that out very quickly. It was traveling from the direction of the North Pole. This means it was likely coming from the USSR. So we immediately reported our findings. My thoughts were that those

Russians had come up with the biggest plane ever. I mean you could launch planes off their wings. (laughter). I had never seen anything like this, but deep down I was a little scared. I mean could you imagine what kind of bombs and how many they could hold? With a plane that size it could take out all the major cities in the continent of North America. I was hoping this was just a malfunction of the radar. But there was one other possibility that was extremely frightening to me.

JB   What was that?

RK   We had never seen it coming over from the USSR, but it could have been a tight formation group of bombers. A tight formation could appear as one radar blip of a large size.

JB   How do you determine the size of the radar hit? Isn't it just a green dot on the CRT (cathode ray tube) display? How did you know it was one object, not many?

RK   On the radar screen itself, there are white lines printed on the glass. The radar needs to be periodically calibrated so that the lines correspond to distance. That is how we could measure the distance between planes. So, with this radar hit, I zoomed in to the largest scale possible and took a ruler to the screen to determine the size. But the radar was never intended to measure the size of planes, just the distances between planes or between plans and other places. As for how I knew it was one? Actually I didn't but I always felt it was. If it was multiple planes, the formation would need to be perfect or the radar hit would change shape.

JB How big was the radar hit?

RK That is very hard to accurately determine as I said, the radar was never designed for this purpose. This system was calibrated to determine distances and not sizes. The Radar blip has fuzzy edges when zoomed in this far. Also, there is an accuracy factor of plus or minus a certain amount, which is likely ever more different for sizes as it is for distances. But I measured it at being anywhere from two hundred meters to five hundred meters across at the widest point. This was likely wing tip to wing tip. But I wasn't there to see it. I sure wish I was though.

JB That must have been a scary feeling seeing something this large going across your screen?

RK Oh man, it certainly was and unreal and scary feeling. We had all wondered if and when the Soviets would attack us. It was a different time back then. The fact that we had never seen a craft of that size sure caused me to panic a bit. But we had a Job to do and we did it correctly. I was also watching a commercial plane coming over the arctic. I believe it was coming from England, but I am not sure. At one point I thought they were going to collide, but I was stunned to see the big plane com up behind and then I only saw the radar signature of the commercial plane which was much smaller. I questioned where the Larger signal went. Often Soviet planes would try to sneak in behind commercial craft to hide from our radar. But this thing was so much bigger that I couldn't see how that idea could possibly work. But as I saw nothing else on the screen, I had to follow the protocol and procedures and assume this is what was done.

JB So, what did you do then?

RK We had already reported it and requested some planes to check it out. But we knew it would take some time for them to get there. Cold lake is a long distance away so it would take a long time to reach this target. So between the time we called for the planes, and the intercept time, we just continued to monitor the radar screen. We saw another plane that appeared on a collision course with this radar blip, naturally that concerned us, but they could have had very different altitudes too. Once they merged, we only saw the commercial plane emerge on our screen. So we reported that to the planes from Cold Lake too. We knew the fighter planes would move in behind the commercial plane to see if there was anything there. But they never saw anything at all. So they went to check Devon Island to see if there was a downed aircraft as that was where we saw the two blips merge and the larger one then disappear.

JB What did you learn from them?

RK Not a dam thing. Those bastards never gave you any information after things occurred. We tried to convince them that we needed their information, so we could be better at our Job, but they didn't buy that. Sad, because it is actually the truth.

JB What happened after that?

RK I was asked for the precise coordinates for the last known location of the large radar return. It is hard to be super precise as things do not always fall strait down. But I could give them a decent generalized area. I believe the planes went first to check on the commercial plane, but not finding anything trailing them, they then went to the last known location to check it out and see what they could find. This was over the south-west part of Devon Island.

JB What makes you think that?

RK Think that it was Devon Island, or what the planes did next?

JB What the planes did.

RK I think that would be the logical thing for the air force to do. There is likely a protocol in the event of a possible downed aircraft: Especially one that would not report a mayday to us or maybe none at all. But we also did continue to observe them on the radar, and they did fly right over that spot.

JB That makes sense. So that radar return was very strange?

RK You think this radar image was strange, what happened next was really screwed up. I got a call from Ottawa that said that everyone at our DEW-Line building was to write an incident report. Even the guys who were asleep during the whole time needed to produce one detailing that they were asleep the entire time. What the hell was that for? I had never heard of this action before. And furthermore we were forbidden from talking to one another about this, and not just for writing the reports, but in the future as well. I mean forever. These reports more accurately resembled an affidavit. I felt like I was signing the Magna Carta it was so important to them.

JB Did you guys talk to one another?

RK Dam straight we did. (Laughter) We were a tight knit group and we talked all the time. This was a strange event for all of us. At the time we were terrified by this. Remember, we thought it was a long-range Soviet Bomber of unheard-of size. It scared the shit out of us. I mean if this thing had reached metropolitan areas, would there have been a home to go to? Back then the ICBM's were in their infancy and the payloads were relatively small compared to what a long-range bomber could carry. Imagine what a plane this size could transport. It would have a huge capacity for bombs and likely a very impressive defence system in place.

JB So what did you eventually learn about this craft?

RK Mostly rumors. Lots of rumors. But one of the guys there did get an interesting letter in the mail. We got our mail one day and this guy, I will call him Paul, got an envelope. He read it and then we were shocked to see him pull out his lighter and burn it up. We asked him about this, and he told the rest of us that there was talk that what we had found was an alien space craft that went down on Devon Island. Now remember that Devon Island is where we saw the radar signatures cross. I have no idea why it went down, and no first-hand knowledge about it. But the date and time quoted by Paul corresponded to what happened on that shift. So obviously something happened there.

JB What rumours did you hear?

RK A few actually. One of the first rumors was that there were living aliens found and brought out. Later rumors were that they (the aliens) were held captive and subject to all sorts of experiments and test. If they did find aliens, and they were subject to the experiments, the poor devils should never have to go through that. But I don't hold much faith in these rumors.

JB Actually, as difficult as it is to believe this, from my research there certainly were some aliens recovered, along with some deceased ones too. Plus they recovered a spacecraft as well. You may be happy to know that from my interviews, I don't believe that the aliens were harmed or held as prisoners. But they were housed in a secure location for their safety. And they were studied too.

RK Really? Are you bull-shitting me? Wow. At least I am so glad to hear that they were treated well. I had wondered if this was true, yet never really believing it was. I thought it if was, I would fear the worst for them if the rumors of their treatment were true. But I didn't really know that there were actual aliens recovered, it was just rumors and I am not sure I ever believed them. Probably more like I didn't want to believe them. Actually, I knew nothing for sure, you can't trust rumors and the military sure isn't going to share their knowledge with me. But the way they handled it only helped to convince me that there was much more to this.

JB Did you ever see other radar returns like this?

RK Never before or since October 4th 1966. But I did hear that there was one a year later to the very day somewhere on the East Coast. But I also heard that it was not as big as the one I saw. Obviously, I cannot give anything more than hearsay on it.

JB I believe that was an entirely separate UFO sighting. I have heard of it too. On October 4th, 1967. I will read up on that one and see if there is any connection to yours.

RK Let me know what you find. I am still trying to figure this all out. It still seems almost surreal to me, especially with the new information you just confirmed. And what is with October 4th anyway? First Sputnik, the Avro Arrow project was announced on the same day. This spacecraft and then another on the following year? Seems odd that it all happens on October 4th.

JB I will also look into any possible connection to that date. Maybe it has something to do with were Sputnik was in relation to the orbit of Earth. Because all of these events the Earth would be in the same place? You never know. As you know from my work in the military, I had access to some weird radar returns in Mount Cheyenne when I was assigned to NORAD for a bit.

RK So we did similar work?

JB Not really, I was doing radio monitoring of weak signals for the military. My actual degree is in electrical engineering. So, was there anything that occurred later that was suspicious to you?

RK After I rotated out of the DEW line, almost one year later, I was brought into a building for what I was told was routine debriefing questions. All I can say about that meeting is 'routine my ass'.

JB   What did that routine debriefing entail?

RK   Nothing much, but more interesting than the questions was who was present for the debriefing. This is why I say it was not routine. Not one of my superiors was actually there, but there was a Brigadier General who I don't recall the name. Something like Cole, I think.

JB   Kornago?

RK   It may have been. Too long ago for me to remember for sure.

JB   Who else was there?

RK   There was a civilian in a suit; at least I think he was a civilian, I don't really know for sure. And there was a retired American General. You might have heard of him, retired General Curtis Lemay. He oversaw the American long-range bomber program called SAC or Strategic Air Command.

JB   He was also believed to be involved in studies of aliens and alien technologies as well. Like Project Blue Book I think, although I do not believe he was part of that group. They called themselves 'Majestic twelve'.

RK   I did hear that too.

JB   Could it have been Brigadier General Mouldy?

RK I don't recognise that name. So probably not. I think it was that name you just gave, Kornago.

JB Did you wonder why General Lemay was there?

RK I didn't at all. I wasn't sure if it was a large long-range Soviet bomber, so him being there made complete sense to me. But after I heard the rumours of what it was, and I learned about his involvement in alien matters, it made even more sense to me.

JB Has the military ever contacted you about anything since your release from the forces?

RK Never, nothing at all. Just prior to my release I did have some extensive paperwork to sign as well as my refresher on the importance of keeping secret issues secret. There was even a hint of intimidation regarding it. But since my release date and my last time in uniform, I have heard nothing more and as so many years have gone by, I am now eighty-one years old, I doubt I will hear anything more.

JB I want to thank you for taking to time to talk with me today. And I would like to take you up on your offer for the note books you kept. It will greatly assist me in writing my book to get the time lines correct. And once again I would like to assure you that your anonymity will be my priority in telling this story.

RK My pleasure and thank you.

Chapter Twenty

Interview with Lieutenant Colonel Douglas Logan

JB   Thank you for meeting with me here today. I wish to assure you that I will not publish this with your real name.

DL   My pleasure. I am happy to hear that my name will be changed for your book as I am sure this is all still top secret.

JB   I am sure it is too. Before we begin, can you tell me why you decided now that you can talk about this?

DL   Sure. All the important players are dead. There are no aliens left so I am not risking their safety. As for the parts of the craft and the alien items, I have no idea where they are, but I am sure they are not in Suffield any longer. Sure, there are technological secrets, but I can keep those to myself and talk about the aliens. I feel it is something we should know about. I mean, we are not alone in this universe. This changes so much with so many people around the globe.

JB   Can you tell me how this all started for you and your crew?

DL   It began in late September of 1966, I was a young captain with the PPCLI back then and we were in Calgary practicing reaction to effective enemy fire for several days straight. We practice until we do it without even thinking about it. We were infantry, so this is a very important procedure that we would practice and practice, and then we practice some more. I think it was early morning of October 5th when I got woken up very early and briefed that I was going to be heading with my team to Devon Island within hours. I was told this was not an exercise and that we would be issued full arctic kit including arms and ammunition. I was told it may be an experimental aircraft from the USSR and that it likely had nukes. We were to capture survivors, treat wounded, and secure the site. Within half an hour or waking up, I have my group formed up and advised. Then we scrambled to get our kit together and it was off to the plane.

JB What were you told of the reason to go?

DL As I mentioned, my briefing was that there was likely a new Soviet Bomber that had gone down on Devon Island. Of course, we were concerned that they may try to blow up the aircraft and possibly try to take some of us with them. So, we came prepared for a fire fight and casualties. There was also a concern that if they had nukes on the plane, they might detonate them and take everything out. We had no idea. So, we were scared that it could blow up and we would never even know. So, our primary objective was to secure the plane and to capture possible Soviet nukes and last was to capture prisoners. We also learned once we got to our plane that this was the biggest aircraft ever recorded. It was seen on the ground by the fighter planes who confirmed that it was massive. We had no idea what we were about to get in to. But we were young and loved the excitement.

JB I can see why that would be scary. What happened when you arrived at Devon Island?

DL We were proceeded by the Canadian Rangers.

JB Just for my record, can you explain who they are?

DL Sure, the Canadian Rangers are a reserve component of the Canadian Forces that are made up of Inuit and first nations members throughout remote locations across Canada. Often, they can be the first ones on the scene of plane crashes or other incidents as they have people all over the Arctic as well as smaller communities in the territories and remote parts of the provinces. They were formed at the start of the cold war as a first line of defence against communist aggression. These men are dedicated and hard workers who do so much for such little remuneration.

JB You talk about the Canadian Rangers quite fondly. You obviously had good experiences with them?

DL I had no experiences with them before this incident, nor after this whole operation was over. This was my one and only time working with them. But I worked alongside them for just a couple days short of one year. That is a very long time to be working side by side. These guys were great. I came in there trying hard not to appear like I am a full-time soldier who knows it all and they were just volunteers who get a free bolt action rifle for signing up. But I quickly learned that they knew many things I did not know.

JB Like what?

DL Besides being very hard workers, they are so knowledgeable about the terrain in which they live in. They know how to not only survive, but how to survive comfortably in the most hostile environments this country could throw at them. We learned so much from them.

JB Such as?

DL I had no idea that in extremely low temperatures you are more likely to get frostbite on your feet when walking on rocks then you would be walking in snow. We trusted our issued equipment, but we quickly learned we had problems. The Rangers broke our wooden pallets and strapped the boards to the bottom of our boots. This helped keep the feet from losing heat to the rocks. There are parts of Devon Island that are an arctic desert, so despite it being extremely cold, there was little or no snow. And because there was no snow, we didn't think of getting our winter mukluks issued to us. We got them on the first equipment drop.

JB So you had a good working relationship with them?

DL Not at first, my men came across a bit arrogant, but it didn't take them long to realise that they had skills we didn't. And they proved themselves as being very hard workers. At first, I had to reassure my PPCLI staff that we could learn so much from them. And we sure did.

JB So what happened when you arrived on Devon Island?

DL The Rangers were the first to arrive, not only on Devon Island, but to the crash site as well. They had a flank covered for several hours. We got a situation report or a sit rep as we call it, from them upon our arrival. It seemed a little too unbelievable; I mean the descriptions of the craft. But there it was. I mean how could a doorway or hatch just disappear into the fuselage of the plane? We couldn't find the hammer and sickle painted on it at all, and we looked. We also checked for other insignia in case it was Chinese. Nothing. I was certain that this was Soviet. And it scared me that they had something this big that could fly so far.

JB So what happened when you first discovered the Aliens?

DL That was weird. The Rangers told us what they saw. I wondered if they ate too much polar bear. It didn't sound right at all, and frankly I didn't believe it. But they were correct and in a few days we saw them too. I had no idea that they could input feelings into my mind. But they did. So, I felt a peace and a calm that I probably shouldn't have felt. Logically I would have been normal for me to have felt intense fear, but I didn't. It wasn't until I walked away back to camp that I realized that I was now terrified. And being terrified is a much more realistic feeling to experience when you first encounter alien life forms that you do not know what their intent is.

JB   Did the Rangers appear scared.

DL   Not until the aliens stopped imputing calm feelings into our minds, and then we were all scared. None of us more so than me.

JB   Why is that?

DL   At that point I had walked away and was no longer under their mind control. Also, I realized that my crew at then were under their thought control. That is a very scary feeling. I was worried that while I was gone, something would happen to them.

JB   When we previously talked, you told me you asked the aliens not to do the mind control, correct?

DL   Absolutely. But I did not want them to stop the mind control until I had the opportunity to advise them of this first. I wanted to explain it to them because I was afraid that my soldiers may end up doing something we would all regret later. Fear can be a very strong emotion.

JB   How did that go?

DL   As soon as they returned to the camp, I could see that they were scared. The mind control seemed to only work a distance, and now they were free from it. I explained this to them, and they were also open to possibilities. I was worried someone would be trigger happy, but fortunately there was never an issue. I had learned though that someone had tried to shoot, but their rifle wouldn't function. I also learned that they (the aliens) had a control system that prevented our weapons from working. That was one of their technologies we had tried to replicate, but only with limited success. I believe the Israelis are working on this system now and that they are having success at close ranges with it.

JB   But your trust was gained, and friendships were made, correct?

DL   We made some lifelong friendships in the case of those who chose to work with the aliens after that first year. Look at me and Scara, we were friends right until he passed away. I felt like I had lost a brother. And that sadness has never really left me.

JB   I am so sorry to hear that. Were there any inappropriate relationships that had developed between the aliens and any of your men? Either PPCLI or the Rangers?

DL   By Romantic, do you mean romance, or do you mean something sexual?

JB   Well, yes. To both actually. (slight laughter).

DL   There was certainly an attraction between a female alien and one of our soldiers that we called Cook.

JB   What happened?

DL   Actually I never found out for sure. I had warned Cook about possible dangers with having intimate contact with the aliens. We did not understand their biology. And that is a concern. What about exposure to unfamiliar bacteria or viruses that may be normal to the aliens? Cook had never indicated if there was any physical intimacy between them, but I am certain there was emotional intimacy. He basically admitted that to me. What I never learned was if she, the alien, had implemented these thoughts into Cooks head, or were they originating from him on his own. I guess I will never know.

JB   Cook died not long after that, right?

DL   Yes, he certainly did, and there were suggestions from the team that he may have got a disease from the alien female. Of course, being dead now, we will never know, the results of the autopsy showed a type of pneumonia that is not too common I understand. Of course, we never told the doctors, or anyone for that matter, that there was a small chance that cook had sex with the alien female. We actually had a small laugh about the possibility. But Cook would have liked that. I understand they cremated him. That was unfortunate as I believe he wanted to be buried. But I guess there was concern of virus or something not from this world. I don't really know, I can only speculate why.

JB   I would like to ask you to describe the physical looks of the aliens for me please.

DL   Sure, they were short, compared to us that is. I would say the average one was about four feet two inches tall. The shortest one was about three and a half feet tall and the tallest one was just less than five feet tall. You know what typical grays look like on movies? Grey hairless creatures with a huge head and big eyes.

JB   Yes.

DL   These guys had similar bodies and heads, but the eyes and skin color was not the same. Their skin was greyish, but much more like human skin. Human like skin with a greyish tint perhaps.

JB   And what about their eyes?

DL   Their eyes were far more human in shape, but much bigger than ours. And their vision was far more acute in low light than ours too. They were hairless on their heads and pretty much just peach fuzz on their bodies. No eyebrows, nor hair in their armpits.

JB   Ok, I have a strange question for you. I don't mean to embarrass you with my next question, but did you observe any alien genitalia? I am aware that experts in anatomy were hired to study them.

DL   Over the years, I certainly did. They were pretty much hairless, although they did have what we would call peach fuzz in place of pubic haid. And the males had a penis that more resembled a cross between a human one and a rat tail. To us it was an ugly thing. But to them I guess it was normal. Males did not have nipples on their chests like human males do. But the women did. They didn't have breasts, but I understand that during pregnancy they do grow and stay engorged until the child is no longer nursing. But as none of them had offspring, I can only tell you what was told by them to us.

JB   In your time at Suffield, did you ever get the chance to observe the lower female genitalia on them?

DL   Not often, but I did learn some things.

JB   Could you tell me what you did see and what you learned?

DL   Of course. The outer area had a similar resemblance to human females, but completely hairless, other than the previously mentioned peach fuzz. The area I believe from reading the reports is called the mons-pubis; it secreted a fluid during stimulation, as did the vagina. So really there were more similarities than differences. This fluid acted as a lubricant not only for the vagina, but also to stop skin on skin chafing. This was all according to the reports from the expert hired to do the anatomical studies.

JB Do you know if the aliens were having sex?

DL You mean with each other, right?

JB Yes. (laughter)

DL I am certain they were, but we respected their privacy. Therefore, I can only guess. But I am guessing yes.

JB How did they prevent pregnancy?

DL I am not certain about that either, but I suspect they were past their child bearing years. But I am guessing at this because I have no idea how things age with them in a normal lifespan.

JB I will switch topics now. I imagine the work at Devon Island was immense. What was involved in breaking down the space craft?

DL That was a logistics nightmare for me, and near never-ending work for the soldiers. I had to be on top of coordinating the arrival or equipment and tools, in addition to needed supplies, and anticipate things before they happened. We had cutting torches, welding equipment, and as none of us were welders, we used the members who took shop courses in high school. We had to teach ourselves with books on the fly. Then there was the metal making up the body of the craft. At some places, the cutting torches would melt too much metal, so we had someone contact a metal fabrication shop for advice. They said we should use a water cutting tool. A high pressure very fine stream to cut metal. I had never heard of this, and there was not much water on Devon Island. Although it was cold, it is an arctic desert.

JB   But you got it done?

DL   We certainly did. We then took each section and either welded metal loops or used a seatbelt like strap to allow a helicopter to lift the section out. Of course, it was all wrapped in tarps, so the pilots would not know what they were lifting.

JB   I know that the PPCLI soldiers were there from start to finish. How about the volunteers from the Canadian Rangers?

DL   As I had already mentioned, those guys were fantastic. They never complained about being called into service for so long. They had spent so much time away from their families. Let's not forget that they were already away from their homes for a couple weeks before they were called up. A couple of them did get to go back to their village to take care of some personal matters, but they came back shortly after that. I think one of the Rangers wives has a child while he was away on Devon Island.

JB   Wasn't this a big hardship on their families?

DL   I am certain that their wives and children missed them very much. But the military made sure that their families had all their needs taken care of as their husbands were working with us. And as they were now working for us, they received deployment pay, so at the end of the year, they had quite a bit of money to return home with. Still, one year away from family is a hardship on anyone. But they never once showed it in their attitudes. Like I said, these guys were great. I have never met anyone like them for their relaxed attitude.

JB   I am assuming during that year, you had staff that was either injured or ill?

DL   Amazingly enough, we had no real illnesses other than Cook. As for injuries, we had a few minor ones. Small burns from welding, the odd hammered thumb. We had minor cuts and bruises. Our medical guy who we called 'Doc' did occasionally release someone from duties for a day or two, but that was uncommon. Actually, we are very lucky we had no other injuries.

JB   When the year was done, did you think this would be the end of your involvement with this project?

DL   That was the longest year of my life as far as being away from civilization and comforts. I thought we would be deployed to the arctic for a few days to maybe one week. And we were there without leaving for one year. So, when we got back, I knew we would all be given some R and R. (Rest and relaxation which is also known as leave). But that never happened right away. Don't forget there was a real concern that if we didn't get the tasks done before the next freeze, there was all likelihood we could have been there another year. Although, there was nothing else we could have done during the freeze time, so we could have rotated staff out on a break. But naturally I am glad we accomplished all our goals before the winter set in.

JB I am glad you achieved your goals in that year. It could have been far worse for you all. What did happen when you arrived at Suffield?

DL As me and my crew were nearly the only ones who knew about the aliens, and the only ones familiar with them, we had to set up their home before we could go on our leave. It makes sense looking back. But we were all overdue for a holiday. We couldn't take them all at once, so a few of us, myself included, offered to stay on for a few more weeks before our turn for vacation came.

JB When did you and your team first learn about the offer to stay on in this program?

DL   Within a few days of our arrival to Suffield. I knew right away that this is something I wanted to do. Most of us did. But there were a couple who wanted out.

JB   Did most make a career out of their new duties?

DL   Yes, one person, we will call him Smith, was fired for talking about the technologies we were discovering. He should have known better. I believe the government gave him enough warning about not to do this again, as we never heard more from or about him. But we all had to attend a meeting about the importance and secrecy of our work. The funny part is that the person who gave the lectures likely had no idea what we did or what our secrets were. We all had a laugh at that.

JB   What was the work like for those who chose to continue working with the aliens?

DL   Morale was great as we felt we were the only ones in the world with this knowledge. Likely there were others in other countries too, but we were not aware of them. So, we felt pretty special. I assigned each member a primary and secondary task based on their skill sets. We had some who were good amateur photographers who would create pictorial books on the alien technologies, and any attempts at reverse engineering. We had a couple guys who were mechanically inclined who would assist on disassembly and reassembly of alien parts, so the photographers could properly catalogue them. Others were assigned in procurement uses. And of course, everything had a top-secret paper trail that must be kept. We had a pretty good budget and would rarely need to beg for more. As long as we justified the money we needed, it pretty much always came in.

JB   What sort of expenditures caused problems?

DL   Comfort things like satellite TV reception and a large aquarium for the aliens to have in their common area. We had a harder time justifying them, but we did get them in the end. I think that Brigadier General Kornago had something to do with this. He seemed to understand the need to keeping the Aliens happy and healthy. I am not sure if he cared for them the way we did, but he knew that we needed to keep them happy for us to continue to get their assistance on all the projects. So the money for these things came in.

JB   When did you first come to appreciate the seriousness of this entire operation and project?

DL   This was probably right after I had put in the request for the custom tent. That thing must have cost a fortune and it was approved almost immediately. And that was the same for everything I had put requests in for. This was highly unusual and would only happen if it was of the highest security or biggest need. Even the request for dozens of cartons of cigarettes for the rangers was approved. They sure loved their cigarettes. We were far happier with receiving beer. Sure there was a couple of my PPCLI staff who liked to smoke too.

JB   Sometime in the nineteen seventies there was a security incident. Could you please tell me about that?

DL   The political situation here in Canada at that time was much different from now. Our Prime Minister was Pierre Elliot Trudeau, and there were terrorist activities going on in Canada, mostly in Quebec by a group called FLQ, I can't recall what the letters stood for. *(Front de liberation du Quebec or in English Quebec Liberation Front).* Trudeau implemented the war measures act which basically enacted marshal law here in Canada. So many soldiers were called up for other duties. We in Project Overshot were working under the name of PPCLI as a cover only. Sure, we wore PPCLI insignia, but we were an autonomous unit. But most bureaucrats didn't know this, and we all got called to head off to Quebec to assist in patrolling the streets. Naturally we were needed in our primary Jobs to take care of the aliens and could not simply head away from our normal duties.

JB   What did you do?

DL   Well, I was scrambling to get in touch with my superior in Ottawa. But I could not get through. I am certain he was very busy in his meetings over the entire FLQ crisis. So, during that time I had no choice but to place one of our staff on the injured list so he could arrange the food and other issues for the aliens. He wasn't sick or injured, but I had to do something. So, I had forged the papers of the doctor. I knew I could be accused of wrong doing, but I also knew that a call to my superior in National Defence Headquarters would end any investigation or discipline right away. I did what I needed to do. Finally, within a very short time before boarding the plane to Quebec, likely a few minutes from take-off, my superior in Ottawa was contacted and he ordered that we stay behind. So, we could now continue to do our Jobs properly.

JB So keeping them happy was a big priority?

DL Keeping them happy and healthy was my number one priority. I really liked these visitors. They had good hearts and great minds. They knew they were living like prisoners, but they never held that against us. They understood why. In addition, we tried to get them anything that would make their time more enjoyable. This included hi-fi stereos, shortwave receivers, and televisions. Snacks of all sorts were provided, plus other kitchen supplies in their private area.

JB Were the aliens happy?

DL As far as I could tell, under the circumstances yes, they were. But we all know that given the opportunity they would have preferred to be free in their home planet. Who wouldn't? But considering they were stuck here, and they knew we would do anything for them that we could, they appreciated it and that helped to make them happy.

JB That's a good point. There was a security breach at one time wasn't there? Could you please tell me what transpired that made this a big concern for you and your section?

DL I am not sure if there actually was. There was some nutcase from Saskatchewan who claimed Canada had a captured Nazi UFO. Naturally this raised some eyebrows of those of us in the know. But fortunately to the rest of Canada he was simply viewed as a holocaust denying moron.

JB That was Ernst Zundel, right? He was the guy who claimed that the holocaust was a concept created by Jews to get fake sympathy?

DL Correct. So, we had to re-vet all the staff of Project Overshot once again, and this was not cheap or easy. But in the end, it was determined that he didn't have any inside information. Coincidently, not long after his claims, a world war two Nazi remote unmanned weather station was found in the arctic. I believe it now resides in the National War museum in Ottawa. But this had nothing to do with UFO's or anything to do with what we were doing in Suffield.

JB	Was there any other security concerns or breaches?

DL	There was always the ongoing talk from staff on Suffield base from those who had nothing to do with Overshot. But those were just simply rumors and we didn't give them much thought. Actually, some of it was very entertaining.

JB	What sort of rumors did you learn about?

DL	Suffield base worked on some biological and possibly even chemical weapons back in the day. Maybe they still do, I don't know. Anyway, it was believed that in the old bunker we kept monkeys that together with the US government; we allegedly developed AIDS for the purpose of eradicating homosexuals. Others believed we were working on chemicals that could be released and may eve cause mind control. Still others said we had aliens, which we did, but they really didn't know that. I am not even sure they really believed that. But it was funny to listen to.

JB	So it was just a lucky guess?

DL	That's right. Coincidently a group of people further north in Alberta built an alien landing pad in 1967. It had nothing to do with our work, and they knew nothing about it. But we all had a good laugh at it. I think it may still be there.

JB	I understand that Major Stefanic arranged a bus tour. Please tell me about that.

DL   We had just managed to bring him on board Project Overshot and he wanted to do something for him to gain their trust as well as something to help the morale of all. So, he talked to me about getting permission to do the bus trip. I said we would need contingency plans for everything, and he would need to put in hours upon hours to create an operations order for this. I submitted it up the chain of command and sometime later they came back with a few more questions. Major Stefanic worked on those revisions and got the entire day trip approved.

JB   What happened next?

DL   I had suggested that we call a meeting of our staff to discuss the trip prior to telling the aliens. Everyone loved the idea, so we called for a meeting in the aliens' common room. Major Stefanic conducted the meeting and then asked the big question, who wants to go on an all-day bus trip. Well everyone there was elated. So, the task began. We modified a bus and contacted all other sections that would need to be utilized. There was so much excitement going on there. You should have seen it. It was like they had renewed energy.

JB   How long did all this planning take once it was approved?

DL   Only a couple weeks. Everyone was so excited about it. Major Stefanic even acted as a tour guide explaining what they were seeing when looking out the bus's windows. The aliens were glued to the glass with excitement and a renewed energy for this outing. I was so impressed with Major Stefanic I had known I made a good call bringing him into the project.

JB You retired not to long after that?

DL Not right away, but my retirement was on my mind. I had put in many years with the military and seen many changes along the way. I had fought bureaucracies and my government in my attempts to look after our alien friends. I had won some battles and lost some battles. Fortunately I won many more than I lost. But in the end though, I was tired, and I wanted to retire. I loved them like a family, so it wasn't an easy decision for me to make. But I knew it was the right one for me.

JB I can imagine. What did you do?

DL I started working on the hand over control of the project to Major Stefanic even before I was certain when I was going to retire. I knew I wouldn't be there forever, and it was a good contingency to have him fully on board regardless of my final date.

JB And once the decision to retire was made?

DL I had decided on a date and I was not going to change it for anything. I knew if I did, it would make walking away even harder on me. How do you walk away from a family? This was like permanently saying good bye to your adult children. I loved them all like family. This was so hard for me to do. I am not even sure they understood to concept of retiring and I feared that they would feel rejected by me. I had to explain it to them that this is something we do. They claimed to understand.

JB What did you do after retirement?

DL I walked off the base and never looked back. It was so hard to do. But I purchased some ocean front property in Sooke, British Columbia. It is on Vancouver Island. So peaceful and quite there. I had my retirement home built and have lived there ever since. We have deer walking on our lawn regularly, and I can look out over the ocean and see the ships come in. Sometimes I even see whales swim by.

JB Did you ever hear more from your alien friends or your military coworkers after you left CFB Suffield?

DL Occasionally I would get a postcard from some of them, both military and aliens, and they were always careful look like nice messages from long ago friends. So even if they were intercepted, it wouldn't contain anything that could be classified. Other than perhaps some odd names. I would always write back but in time the post cards became fewer and fewer. I know that the aliens have now all died off. It is very sad, I loved these people. There are still some soldiers who are still around. But age is setting in. I am seventy-seven now. I have seen Major Stefanic a handful of times though. He was moved to CFB Esquimalt after Project Overshot shut down.

JB   Do you know what happened to Project Overshot?

DL   I believe that all the physical items, all the files and photographs, and even the remains of the alien bodies have been placed in a large government storage repository.

JB   Have you ever returned to the Arctic?

DL   Never. I should have when I was younger, but I am too old for that now. It would have been nice to visit, especially as a reunion from our group and the Rangers.

JB   Have you remained in touch with any of them?

DL   Sadly none of the Rangers, as for our group in Project Overshot, just Major Stefanic. I do not hear from anyone in our PPCLI group.

Chapter Twenty-One

Interview with Major Stan Stefanic

JB Thank you for taking the time to meet with me today. I want to assure you of your anonymity on this project of mine. Your true name will never be revealed by me. I am not even writing my books using my real name. That way it protects us both.

SS It is my pleasure. And thank you for your assurance. I could be in real trouble if it was learned that I am giving you this interview. I hope I can be of assistance to you and your book.

JB I am sure you will be most invaluable to me. So as the last person in charge of Operation Overshot...

SS Project Overshot.

JB Right sorry, Project Overshot. As you were the last person in charge of Project Overshot, how come you decided to come to talk with me now after you had first declined?

SS You first contacted me after getting my information from Lieutenant Colonel Logan (*Not his real name, changed in the transcript by the author*). When I first heard from you it was quite unexpected, I was not exactly happy pleased to be hearing from you. As you may recall?

JB Yes, I do recall that. But I did contact you out of the blue without you being aware. So it is natural that your training would kick in and you wouldn't want to talk. But you eventually came to change your mind. If I may ask, how come your change of heart?

SS Actually I was downright pissed off with you, to be completely honest. But then I thought about it more. It was at that time that I thought that it might be good for the public to hear about what truly went on here in Canada. In the last couple years of Project Overshot, we joked that on our little corner of CFB Suffield, we were just like Area 51. And as you likely know, all the aliens have now passed away. So, they will not be in any danger whatsoever.

JB Well I actually didn't know that they had all passed on. I suspected that they might have, but I really wasn't sure. But it has been a few years now. Not that I am any expert on their life span. But I am sorry to hear it.

SS Thank you. After the last one passed on, we took all the equipment, all the parts of the space ship, and all remnants of the project and locked them in deep storage. That took almost one year. This effectively is what led to the end of Project Overshot. The closing up took about one year, and I was eventually moved to CFB (*Canadian Forces Base*) Esquimalt. I resumed my legal career with the military there for about five more years. That is when I decided to retire. So, I guess that part of the story can come out now.

JB But this entire project, from its inception of discovery at Devon Island through to the last of it being sent out to the secured storage is still top-secret right?

SS As far as I am aware, it is still classified as top secret. I may be guessing, but I think it may always be. When I left the military, I had an exit interview that included all the usual and standard comments about maintaining military secrets for ever. I had to laugh inside because as a former JAG officer (military lawyer) I was the one often drafting the non-disclosure agreements for the military, now I was the one signing it.

JB Could you please tell me what was it like when you were first being brought into the project? You know, learning all about these secrets, all the technologies, meeting the aliens?

SS Oh man, you wouldn't believe it. When I first came to the military after law school, I was feeling like some young hot shot military lawyer who was ready to court martial the chief of defence staff himself. (Laughter) I thought I had seen it all and knew it all. I tried not to come across all cocky, and maybe I gave off the right impressions, but that is who I was inside. Outside, I tried to be cool and relaxed. So, I thought I was pretty special and with an ego that big, when you are approached to be involved in something top secret, you think to yourself, well who else could they possibly choose? I was such an arrogant ass back then. But I knew how to keep a secret and I also knew not to act so arrogant. But a few years later in my career, with the occasional ass chewing from above and the ego quickly goes away. Then a few years later with the Project Overshot well underway, you see the building and you hear the wild rumors, and you never think you will be brought in to this project. Then out of the blue, I was consulted and became peripherally part of the project. But when I learned of the full details of the building, I suddenly felt really small. I realised how little I must really know. And I was humbled for being brought in on this project. The aliens were great. Not a trace of arrogance in them. I think it was them that made me a better person. It was impossible for me not to want to do everything I could for them. They were so nice to everyone. The always instilled a feeling of appreciation for everything you did for them. It made me want to do even more for them. I had never seen them get annoyed or angry with each other or anyone else for that matter. The most easy going group I have ever met.

JB How were you sure they were not using their mind control on you in order to get things they wanted?

SS Looking back, I think they were. But they never abused it. I think it was their way of showing appreciation and manners, because they would otherwise not know how human manners worked. So, we all liked doing things for them. Even if it was mind control, so what? Appreciation is appreciation, and they appreciated us. We have to stop thinking like humans here. We need to try to understand their ways. So, I always tried to accept their ways as a positive thing. Actually, I really believe this about them. We could easily view it as mind control, but I don't think that is what they intend at all.

JB   I heard that you arranged to take them out on a bus trip for a few hours to Calgary?

SS   That's correct. It was a real challenge. Getting approval, assuring the headquarters that the security risk was low. Convincing them that the aliens had no intention of escape. The list went on and on. And then there was all the planning around the actual bus trip. We had unmarked military police vehicles there to stop the RCMP (Royal Canadian Mounted Police) or a municipal police force from stopping us and from searching the bus. We had the best driver we could find, and the bus was modified so that you could look out, but not in, and also so the driver could not see who he was transporting.

JB   Who did the driver think he was driving?

SS   He believed he was taking a group of British Soldiers on a bus tour of Calgary. He never enquired about the secrecy, only commented that they must be important due to all the security. He was right, they were very important.

JB Why did he think they were British soldiers?

SS Suffield base had been used by the British for many years, I think they still are there. This was the training area Canada traded for the hulls of three submarines a number of years ago. Brittan had been using this area for many years.

JB I recall that. Back to the aliens, what was the tour like for them? It must have been a very long day for them?

SS Honestly it was the most amazing time for all of us. They had never seen our cities except from space and on their TV set, and now they were driving down the roads looking up at the tall buildings, seeing the people, the sites, the sounds. It was so much fun watching them watch the city. Sure, they had seen it on TV from their residence inside the old bunker, but this was different. This was real to them. It was one of the most amazing experiences of my life watching them take in the sights and sounds of the highway and Calgary.

JB I bet it was it a long day for them?

SS It sure was, but they were glued to the windows of the bus, looking into other cars on the highway, looking out on the fields and farms, asking a million questions. It was likely the best day they had ever had on earth to this point. And by then they had been here for many years.

JB   Where did you go?

SS   We took them on a road trip to Calgary, then a bus tour of the city and returned back to Suffield. Like I said, it was a very long day.

JB   What sort of things did you show them in Calgary?

SS   Well, the downtown core and all the tall buildings that housed offices. The area from the 1988 winter Olympics. Of course, we showed residential areas as well as shopping malls, etc. By then, we had to head back to Suffield as it was a very long drive. In the evening when dark out, they pretty much all fell asleep. But I was dozing off too.

JB   How close did you get to them?

SS   You mean emotionally?

JB   Yes.

SS   Very. My primary duties for the government were to obtain information and technology. But unofficially, my primary duty, in my mind anyway, was to make the aliens remaining years as happy and as comfortable as possible. They deserved it as they have given so much to Canada, without asking for anything back. I guess that was the biggest thing I learned from the previous officer in charge, Lieutenant Colonel Logan. He was good to them and he loved them like family. I am pretty sure they loved him back too. I developed this relationship with them in time too, which is why he recommended me to take over from him after his retirement.

JB   I am sure they valued your attitude. I mean both the aliens and Lieutenant Colonel Logan.

SS   I hope so, that would help me feel like I did my Job properly. This was so different from the JAG office, or any other office in the military.

JB   When Lieutenant Colonel Logan retired, how did the aliens feel?

SS   There were not too many of them left, under a dozen if I recall correctly. They knew they would never see him again and naturally they were sad about this. I mailed him some simple postcards from them with messages that were likely meaningless to anyone else but him. He mailed some back too. The aliens knew they were from him, and vice versa, so these postcards brought them all some happiness. Still they missed him very much. Actually, it was his idea that I arrange the bus trip. But he didn't tell anyone that as he wanted me to take all the credit for the trip so the transition of me taking over would be smoother. He knew for a long time that he was getting to the point of wanting to retire. He was a good man to all his staff, not just the aliens. He took little to no credit for all the great things he did. But he sure took responsibility for anything that went wrong.

JB What sort of things went wrong?

SS Not very much. Mostly things to do with logistics. Fortunately, there was only little issues to do with security. Although when there was a concern of a security breach, he thought of it as a failure on his part. But as you know, we never actually had a security breach. You see, that was the kind of man he was. He was a true and good leader. We all miss him. He poured everything he had into this project. And all his staff and the aliens knew that.

JB He sounds like a really good man, and I enjoyed my meetings with him. I am sure he was missed by the remaining staff and especially the aliens. So, tell me, what was the mood like after the last alien passed away.

SS When he left, there was a void, he was missed by everyone. As for the aliens, with the passing of each one there was a deep sadness. We all knew there would be a day when they were all gone. But once the second to last one there had passed away, the remaining one became very depressed. We all knew it, we all saw it. I had made arrangements for a staff member to be with her, or in the adjoining room around the clock thereafter so that she was not alone, except by her own choice. I am sure she still felt very alone, but I couldn't sit back and do nothing. Then, only a few short months later she too passed away. It was a very sad day for us all. None of our old friends were left.

JB And that was the end of the project?

SS No, not yet. But it was certainly the beginning of the end. I contacted NDHQ and was given new instructions on what to do.

JB What were those new orders?

SS Obviously there was no more information to be obtained from the aliens, they were all gone. But we still had all the recovered equipment that needed to be dealt with. That, along with over quarter of a million photographs, and literally thousands of files on the alien equipment. This doesn't even include the truckloads of files on the administrative side of all this. This vast amount of data and materials all needed to be placed in a high security storage center. I am not even privy to where this high security storage place is located.

JB How does that work?

SS Well, as for the items held in storage, I know of no one who actually knows where it is.

JB I don't understand.

SS Let me explain that a little better. Those that know the location do not know what the crates contain. And those few who know what the crates contain, do not know where they are located. It is a perfect way of hiding things. There is a list of contents that are included in each crate. This list is the only way of locating items. And this list is locked in secure document storage in Ottawa. And there are likely less than five senior officers with access to this information.

JB As for the storage, it sounds very secure. I guess it needs to be. All that data and materials must have been a few truck loads?

SS A few truck loads? Try a couple hundred truck loads. All of the trucks were carrying secured containers. Honestly, the amount of data and materials is beyond anyone's imagination. Did you ever see the movie 'Raiders of the Lost Ark'?

JB Yes

SS I picture the storage center to look something like the one at the end of that movie. I have no idea how big it is, or where this center is. But with the last shipment out, we were closed down for good. It was a bitter sweet day for all. Of course the cooks and some of the other support staff were released long before.

JB What happened to all the staff?

SS I was lucky, I got an administrative legal position with the JAG office in Esquimalt base in British Columbia. I get to meet with Lieutenant Colonel Logan periodically, as he lives relatively close by over in Sooke. As for the other staff, all the long-term staff had retired. Some retired a few years before, and others after the passing of the last one. But as their numbers declined, so did our numbers. The remaining staff that chose to stay, such as the civilian staff, was absorbed by other places within the Canadian Forces.

JB One last question for you.

SS Yes?

JB Did you ever tell your wife about Operation Overshot?

SS Um, wow. I didn't expect that question. But I guess I can answer this one. Yes, I did. To this day she things I made up the whole story. She doesn't believe a word of it. I can't blame her for that.

Chapter 22

Interview with Brigadier General Mouldy

JB   Thank you for taking the time to see me.

AM   No problem, I have been in this care home for some time now, so any visitors here are greatly welcomed. This isn't how I figured I would spend my retirement years. (Slight laughter)

JB   I can only imagine. I would like to start with some background questions if I may.

AM   Of course.

JB   You were in charge of CFB Suffield for some time back in the mid 1970's?

AM   I was, Back then I was a Colonel and now it is done by a Lieutenant Colonel, or even a colonel, but in the early days of it becoming a Canadian Forces Base, I was there. Now being the rank of Brigadier General, I couldn't run the base, except on an interim basis as I also did in 1985. My time there in the mid 70's was limited to getting the base up and running as prior to 1971 it was only a training area. But as I said, I did come back in 1985 for about six months.

JB   So you oversaw the day to day operations of the base?

AM For the most part. But just on the bigger scale. I don't want to micro manage the place. That is poor leadership.

JB Were you ever made aware of what was going on inside the old bunker of CFB Suffield?

AM Officially no. I heard rumors. But officially nothing; in fact, I was told it was my Job to stop the rumors and that I am never to investigate the bunker, or rumors myself, but just to report them.

JB Did that cause you to wonder even more what was going on?

AM Of course it did, but I knew enough to let it go. Asking too many questions when the higher-ups tell you not too, is not a good career building decision.

JB What things did you hear from the rumors?

AM I heard all sorts of crap. All those weird sorts of things that cause me to want to punish those who spread these stupid stories. There was an old saying, 'If you haven't heard a rumor by noon, start one.' I think this was the philosophy of many staff from Suffield at that time. There were even rumors about me.

JB Ok, let me rephrase this question. What sort of crap did you hear?

AM I heard fantastic stories of aliens being held underground there. I mean really, little green men. What kind of B.S. is that? That was the most common rumor. I always wondered how a base full of logical thinking people could come up with that one. I had the hardest time quashing this rumor too. The other stories were easier to shut down.

JB   What were those rumors about?

AM   Oh, everything from the military was making biological warfare materials in the underground to the stories of an underground brothel. I didn't give any of these rumors any credibility at all. I even heard rumors about me. (Laughing)

JB   What rumors did you hear about yourself?

AM   The best one was that I was an alien reptile. How ridiculous is that? I have no idea where they come up with this shit.

JB   That is different. So, what do you think was going on down there?

AM   That is a great question. Officially I was not to have an opinion, but thinking there were scientists going in and out, plus support staff, I would guess it was some sort of military research. But I have no idea what. The staff employed in Project Overshot were very secretive. I had nothing to do with them or shipments to and from their part of the base. And Ottawa made that very clear to me that I was not to be poking in on their business. One time I was even ordered to have the flag at half-staff, but I have no idea why. I complained, but the staff in National Defence in Ottawa told me to keep it at half-staff. They had some power over there at the bunker. Whatever it was, it was likely a very big deal.

JB And you never did learn what was going on other than the rumors?

AM Never. The military was not about to tell me. It didn't matter to headquarters that I was a senior officer. I didn't need to know therefore I wouldn't get to know. But that is the army way.

JB When your time commanding CFB Suffield came to an end, and you were rotated out, did you continue to hear rumors?

AM I was not really hearing any rumors. But many people asked me about them. So, the rumors were out there.

JB I guess I can't be too surprised. I know how rumors fly in the military.

AM But it was still my job to shut down any rumor I hear. But it seemed that the more I tried to shut them down, the more the rumors came out. Isn't that why you are interviewing me?

JB Partly yes. I learned of the story of aliens being housed at CFB Suffield and thought it be interesting to learn more about it.

AM Then you are just as bad as all the others.

JB What do you mean?

AM   There is nothing at all like that going on at Suffield. I may not know everything that went on there, but I would sure know about that. These rumors are nothing more than fear mongering and dangerous. Had I known you are trying to spread this bull shit I would not have agreed to meet with you.

JB   But I am just trying to get both sides of this story.

AM   Listen to me clearly. Those were all just BS rumors and there was nothing going on there at all that involved little green men. It is all bullshit.

JB   Thank you for your time General Mouldy. I really appreciate you taking the time to allow me to visit with you. You have been very informative, and I assure you, I will certainly publish your views in my book, if I decide to publish it.

AM   I am glad you are going to tell the truth. Although I don't think it is worth publishing. It is just a stupid rumor.

JB   Thank you for all your time.

AM   You're welcome.

Chapter 23

Interview with Captain Fred (Black Cloud) Engle, CC130 Pilot

JB Captain Engel: Thank you for taking some time out of your schedule to talk with me today.

FE Please, call me Fred. I haven't been called Captain Engel in so many years. Not since the day I left the Air Force.

JB Okay, Fred it is. Could you tell me how you gained the nick name 'Black Cloud'? I am certain there is a good story there. I am familiar with air force giving nicknames to pilots. I was army for many years, but I spent a good part of my career on an air force base.

FE Many years ago, I guess it was the early to mid-nineteen sixties, it was during an aviation exercise once, I was being followed by our, enemy plane. It was a fellow pilot who was assigned to do the role of enemy that day. So, being pursued by him, I few into a black cloud. And doing this is something we are taught not to do except in an emergency. I messed up by doing this and got stuck with the nickname from then on. We all had a nick name for something we did wrong. Although if it had been a real combat situation, I certainly would have done it again.

JB As we discussed on the phone, you were the pilot who flew many transports from Canadian Forces Base Winnipeg to Devon Island and back, and that was in the mid nineteen sixties?

FE Close. I flew from Winnipeg to Devon Island. Sometimes we did a low and slow airdrop, other times we landed and dropped off and picked up crates. Then my captain and I would fly to Suffield base in Alberta. Typically, we would stay the night there before returning to Winnipeg the next day.

JB I understand that you were the co-pilot and you flew with a captain, so you and your captain were the only ones that flew these missions there during this time?

FE Yes, right up until the end, that was mostly true. There were also a couple helicopter pilots who picked up large items with their Chinook. But they were much closer as a Chinook can't travel anywhere near as far as our plane.

JB Besides the helicopter, why were you and your captain the only ones to fly to Devon Island at this time?

FE I was told it was of the highest security, so they didn't want to bring anyone else into the operation of whatever was going on there. We never did learn what was going on there.

JB What was the purpose of all of those flights?

FE   In a broad sense, it was to drop off crates and pick up crates from a remote bivouac on Devon Island. All very hush hush though.

JB   Did you know what was in these crates?

FE   I do not have a clue. And I knew I wasn't supposed to ask. Our load tech knew the weight, and which crate was placed where on the plane based on that crates weight, but that was about it.

JB   Did you ever see what was on the ground there when you flew over that part of Devon Island?

FE   The first few times I saw something that looked like a giant boomerang. It was huge, but after a while it was covered in large tarps that were the same colour as the ground. I had used it as a reference point for flying, but once covered I could no longer do that. Fortunately, they had lights set up on a makeshift airstrip.

JB   Do you know, or did you ever learn what that large boomerang shaped object was?

FE   I assumed it was an experimental aircraft. I hoped it was ours, but I learned it was likely Russian. Biggest and oddest-looking plane you have ever seen. The Russians designed a huge plane but obviously it was a failure. Only one flight and it crashed. Likely it was too expensive to keep throwing money at. So, after the crash, they probably cancelled the project.

JB   Do you know if there were any survivors?

FE   I can only assume there were none. At my first landing, I took away some caskets. And over the next few months a couple more. I figured they found some more dead bodies as they dismantled this plane.

JB   So how long did this go on for?

FE   They cancelled all my holidays for the entire year of nineteen sixty-seven but gave them all back in nineteen sixty eight. So, I had a big break the next year that was really enjoyed by my wife Joan and myself.

JB   How long did this operation go on for?

FE   It went on for well over one and a half years. The first half was constantly dropping off supplies and picking up crates of unknown goods. I would fly them to Suffield and back to the circuit again. At about the one-year mark I landed empty and picked up many personnel. I flew them to Suffield and then the next day I was to fly to Edmonton and pick up a whole new crew to take to Devon Island. Over the course of the next one and a half months, I would pick up all the remaining equipment from them and fly it back. My last flight to and from there was to get the remaining crew with the last of their equipment out.

JB   That must have been so many flights.

FE Literally dozens, in under a year and a half. Sometimes even four times a week. I should pull out my old flight longs and add them up. I think did that once and it was about seventy flights.

JB But everything was removed?

FE If I flew you there right now, you would not be able to tell that humans ever set foot there. That is how well cleaned up it was. But I only got off the plane there a couple times. I was told that I should not get off of it. But sometimes I would go for a pee.

JB And just like that the flights were over?

FE Just like that. Then I went on my overdue holidays. Joan, my wife, we were newlyweds back then; her and I went off to Hawaii for a nice long needed break. I needed her forgiveness for being away so much for over one year.

JB I bet that was a much-needed rest time for the two of you.

FE You have no idea. It was our unofficial honeymoon. Our real one was in the summer of 1966, but then I got so busy with work. So, this vacation was very special to me.

JB In all your time doing these flights, were you ever made aware of the equipment you were picking up or dropping off or the significance of the trips?

FE   I knew I was bringing in many tools and generators, also fuel and other standard supplies. There were even parts to build a Quonset hut. There were pumps and hoses, and then there were the standard supplies that you would need for an extended military operation. But I was never told anything of what was going on at Devon Island.

JB   What sort of things did you remove from Devon Island?

FE   Nowhere near as much as I had dropped off. At least not yet. The pieces of the plane were taken out by Chinook. So, I took out a couple bodies during the first year, along with sealed crates, and that is about it. After the original crew was removed, and a second set was brought in, I helped remove all the remaining tools, the pieces of the Quonset hut, all the tents and the remainder of the bivouac site. We left that area as if nothing had ever happened there. I guess they were worried that sometime the Russians would show up looking for their plane.

JB   So as a junior pilot, this must have been fantastic for getting your hours up on your commercial license.

FE   I had many hours in, and I was fortunate. And for the most part those flights were really nice to do. I recall a funny story if you are interested.

JB   Sure.

FE We were flying a CC130 empty of staff except for my pilot and me. Therefore, we ran unpressurized and used air masks. Well, there was a stowaway on board.

JB A Stowaway?

FE Yes, but not what you would think. It was a huge black fly buzzing around the cockpit. Slowly it would pass out from lack of oxygen. I would then remove my facemask and give him a shot to revive it.

JB That is funny.

FE My captain didn't think so. You see this went on probably twenty times. It kept passing out and I kept reviving it. Finally, the captain's hand came out and slapped it dead. We hardly spoke a word to each other the remainder of the day, but inside I was laughing hysterically.

Chapter 23

Interview with Nippikortouok (Brian) 'Big Whistling Moose' Uvlugiaq (McIntyre)

JB   How are you doing? Do you mind if I call you Brian?

BM   For sure. That is my common name. My Inuit name is Nippikortuyok Uvlugiaq which translates loosely to English as 'Loud Stars in the Sky'. Which is pretty much who I am, but most people just call me Brian.

JB   Can I ask you where the nickname 'Big Whistling Moose' had come from? It does paint an interesting visual.

BM   Oh my, I haven't heard that nick-name in quite a few years. The crew on my Canadian Ranger team came up with that name for me years ago. As for the interesting visual, an artist friend of mine carved a big whistling moose for me out of narwhal tusk. There is a long unrelated story on that one.

JB   Will you share that story with me?

BM   No. (laughter) But the name was shortened to just 'the Moose'. After some time. However, they always recalled the long name.

JB   (laughter) Okay then. Is this your hometown, Clide River here on Baffin Island?

BM   Born here and raised here.

JB   How long ago was that?

BM   I believe I was born somewhere around nineteen thirty to thirty two. I am not really sure as We didn't keep much in the way of records back then. (More laughter)

JB   Fair enough. (laughing) So when did you join the Canadian Rangers?

BM   I think it was in nineteen forty seven, right after they were formed. I was a young man back then and I was broke. They gave you a nice rifle for Joining, plus an annual allowance of ammunition too. I even shot a few walruses with that one. (More laughter).

JB   I bet you have. Are they any good to eat?

BM   Are you staying for dinner?

JB   If you are inviting me, I am staying.

BM   Then they are fantastic.

JB   I am looking forward to it. So, back to my questions: Were you old enough to join the Canadian Rangers back in nineteen forty-seven? You were between fifteen and seventeen years of age.

BM   I probably was not old enough. But I never lied when they asked my age. I said I could be seventeen, but don't have an actual date or birth certificate ever issued.

JB   That is interesting. Kind of like the soldiers who signed up during world war one. So how did you come to learned of this mission? By radio?

BM   Me and the other rangers would go on hunts together so that we could also do our ranger work simultaneously. As part of the training, we would check in with a center via the luggable battery powered radio. We did our check in and we were told to go to Devon Island. Once there we were to look for a downed plane and search for survivors and if it was Russian, we were to take it captive. Do you know Devon Island?

JB   No, not really, except on maps. It is a very big place.

BM   It is huge. Fortunately, they gave us some coordinates, or it could have taken us years to find a downed plane. I have actually been there a few times before, and since too. But I have not been there for many years now. There is no need to go there. Hunting is bad on this island. But I have heard that NASA is using a part of it for some research. But I have no idea where.

JB   I do understand it is that big. Actually, I read that it is the twenty seventh largest island in the world.

BM At the time I thought it was the largest. (More laughter).

JB How long did it take you to get there?

BM Only a few hours as the sea was frozen, and we rode the snowmobiles there in relatively short time.

JB So you were not that far away?

BM Coincidently we were pretty close considering the area.

JB What did you do when you arrived at Devon Island?

BM We parked the snowmobiles up high on the coast, along with the sleds we were towing. We took as much gear as we could easily carry and proceeded to hike up the side of the cliffs. They were really high, but once over the top the island slopes gently into a large bowl. It was clear and dark, so it didn't take too long to spot some lights in the direction of the coordinates we were provided with. But it was still a long hike getting to the downed craft. Of course, we advanced on it very carefully believing it was a crashed communist plane.

JB What happened when you got close?

BM We slowed right down and sent some of our rangers to proceed around to the side to cover us when we approached it. We gave them plenty of time to set up before we proceeded to the plane. We noticed that we could not locate the windows or any doors.

And that confused us. There had to be a way in and out and there had to be a way to see outside. We went around the entire craft but could not locate engines, doors, windows, or any other hatch. This was very confusing to us. But we continued to watch the plane for some time before the regular soldiers arrived.

JB What was it like working with them for such a long time?

BM It was very different for us. We try to be jovial in what we do; it is our way up here in the North. The soldiers were all so serious at first. But in time they learned to appreciate our humor, and they even participated in it.

JB I heard that in a very short time you and your team managed to gain their respect.

BM That was our plan. Before we even met up with them, we felt they would look down on our military skills. We were volunteers who were given free rifles. They were professional soldiers. Sure, we know the arctic, but they knew war. So, we learned quite a bit from each other. We actually became pretty good friends over that year.

JB That is fantastic. I heard a story about how you and your team cleared the make-shift runway of all rocks and boulders, basically giving the soldiers a longer break.

BM Naw, we all did that together. We all took a break for dinner and my crew and I went back out to finish the work. Then they Joined us for the last big boulders. It was a busy day there, but we all worked together to get it done. But they like to say we did so much. We only did a bit more work.

JB I also understand one or two of the Rangers went home for a bit?

BM I can't recall why, maybe someone's wife was having a baby, but he was picked up by a Chinook helicopter, dam those things are loud, and they took him away. When he came back, one of the men in his village named Jimmy Iqaluq had carved several stone carvings of polar bears that were given to the aliens. They really loved them, and they seemed so happy with these gifts. I think the soldiers were jealous of the carvings. (more laughter) Perhaps he should have brought more back with him.

JB I bet they were jealous. I know I would be. So, was there ever a concern of Russian soldiers showing up, they likely saw this craft on their radar too?

BM I have no idea, but we were told to always keep our rifles near us when working, and we always had staff up around the clock keeping watch on both the camp and the spaceship. Also, there was always two staff located up on a high point to keep watch for others. We all took turns doing the different tasks. Keeping watch was the worst. But it had to be done. It was so cold on the ridge.

Fortunately, nothing ever happened. I never saw anyone there who shouldn't be there.

JB But you always kept vigilant?

BM Always. You never know. We also by habit watch for polar bear, but we never saw any on Devon Island.

JB Do you feel like you accomplished something important when you were on this deployment?

BM For sure. I may not understand all that has been achieved in my work there, and I may not understand the significance of it. But I do accept I was a key person in something very big. I may even make it to Aurora someday.

JB That is the highest level of Inuit heaven; correct?

BM That it is.

JB Could you explain that to me please?

BM (*taking a book from his shelf, he read*) It is told that the ends of the land and sea are bounded by an immense abyss, over which a narrow and dangerous pathway leads to the heavenly regions. The sky is a great dome of hard material arched over the Earth. There is a hole in it through which the spirits pass to the true heavens. Only the spirits of those who have died a voluntary or violent death, and the Raven, have been over this pathway. The spirits who live there light torches to guide the feet of new arrivals. This is the light of the aurora.

JB Thank you. That was really very nice. You were part of something huge and you gave up one year of your life to work towards it. I think you did a great thing for Canada, its people, and especially for the aliens.

BM Thank you.

JB Do you have any specific stories of your work on this project?

BM Many, where to begin? I guess we could start with the building of the makeshift runway we already talked about. Some of the regular military went to scout where would be the best place. There were many things they were looking for that I would never know due to that work.

JB Likely a long enough flat ground with either no obstacles, or ones that can be easily removed. The direction of the wind, if there were hills behind the runway, the plane would need to be able to clear it on take-off. It would likely be those sorts of things.

BM Makes sense to me. Anyway, they identified where it would be so we all went off to the proposed air strip and formed an extended line that would end up walking the distance. Starting from the center, we passed rocks down the line to clear the runway. The rocks were piled up along the sides of the strip. We worked for many hours clearing this, and all that was left was some huge boulders. At that time, we took a meal break and headed back to the camp. After the meal, we (*the rangers*) slowly one by one left the tent. We proceeded back to the runway to remove the large boulders. Some of these boulders were huge and it took all of use to remove them. We were down to the last one or two boulders when the Pats (*edit note: A nick name for 'Princess Patricia's Canadian Light Infantry or PPCLI*) showed up. The quickly lent a hand on the last two big boulders and we were done. They seemed so happy that we did there after dinner. I think that was a turning point in our work with them. After this, they knew we would work hard and try to have a good attitude.

JB As we already discussed, I had heard about that time. I learned it from Lieutenant Colonel Logan. He said that your work really impressed his men. Do you have any other stories?

BM I have a few from our down time.

JB I would love to hear them.

BM Well we taught both the regular soldiers and the aliens to play some Inuit games. We also gave the aliens some beer. That was funny, but the officer in charge put a stop to it. He was probably right.

JB What happened?

BM   Well it didn't take them much to be drunk, like not even a beer. Then Captain Logan said it was likely because we have different bodies. He was concerned that it could be a poison to them. I think it is a poison to all of us, but we drink it anyway. (Laughing).

JB   What was it like seeing the aliens drunk?

BM   It was very fun to watch. They couldn't stand straight; they were being funny and very happy. Sadly, they were a little sick the next day. But it brought us all closer together. Us Rangers bonded not only with the Pats, but also with our new alien friends. I will remember them fondly until the day I day and see them in Aurora.

JB   I am sure you will.

BM   Thank you.

Manufactured by Amazon.ca
Acheson, AB